EARLY SCOTTISH POETRY

Edited by GEORGE EYRE-TODD

EARLY SCOTTISH POETRY

THOMAS THE RHYMER
JOHN BARBOUR
ANDROW OF WYNTOUN
HENRY THE MINSTREL

GREENWOOD PRESS, PUBLISHERS
WESTPORT, CONNECTICUT

Originally published in 1891
by William Hodge & Company, Glasgow

Reprinted from an original copy in the collections
of the University of Illinois Library

First Greenwood Reprinting 1971

Library of Congress Catalogue Card Number 77-98753

SBN 8371-3094-8

Printed in the United States of America

NOTE.

IT has long been a reproach that, owing to the
absence of an accessible edition, no popular know-
ledge of the early poetry of Scotland was possible
—that, while texts of the early English poets, such as
Chaucer, Langland, and Gower, were within reach of
all, no such facilities were available for the equally
interesting and valuable works of Thomas the
Rhymer, Barbour, Wyntoun, and Henry the Minstrel.
The present volume is an attempt to supply this want.

From their great bulk the works of the poets here
dealt with may with obvious advantage be studied
in selected form. In each case, however, an effort
has been made, by means of summaries between
the selected passages, to afford a view of the entire
poem.

CONTENTS.

EARLY SCOTTISH POETRY.

ONE of the commonest of popular mistakes
upon philological subjects has been the supposi-
tion that the Lowland Scots language was
nothing more than a rude or corrupted dialect
of ordinary English. The making of two
dictionaries and the writing of many dissertations
have not completely dispelled this impression.
Students, however, have long been aware that
the popular idea was mistaken; their only
difficulty has been in ascertaining the actual
origin of the tongue. Dr. Jamieson, in the
earlier Scottish dictionary, was at great pains
to prove the language a dialect of Gothic; and
Dr. Charles Mackay, in his more recent com-
pilation, though right in the main, betrayed
something of a tendency to advocate Gaelic
sources. It is now agreed by those most
competent to judge that the tongue spoken
in the Scottish lowlands was the most northern
of the three great dialects of English. Of these
dialects the southern form, once the language

of Kent and Devon, has now all but entirely died out; and while the midland form, by regular evolution, has developed into the written and spoken English of to-day, the northern, by literary use and from the fact of its national foundation, obtained a permanence in Scotland for at least five centuries. It was the language of court and bar, made golden by the tongues of poets and gentle by the lips of fair dames. There are those yet living who say that in their youth there were few pleasures more delightful than to listen to the talk of some old lady who retained the quaint and noble manner of the "auld Scots tongue." This language possessed a charm unknown to our modern speech. English was admitted by Dr. Mackay to be perhaps the most muscular and copious language in the world, but he remarked that it was harsh and sibilant, while the Scottish, with its beautiful terminational derivatives, was almost as soft as Italian. An Englishman, he said, speaks of a "pretty little girl," a Scotsman of a "bonnie wee lassie."

In course of time, owing to the intimate relations of the Scottish court with France, the language of the northern kingdom became strongly tinctured with French modes of expression. Indeed, finally it came in many respects to resemble the tongue rather of the

country's ally than of its neighbour. The
foreign influence is strongly marked in the
language of Dunbar and the later fifteenth and
sixteenth century poets, and is conspicuous in the
pronunciation of such words as *flours*, more like the
French *fleurs* than the English *flowers*. To the
present day many words in common use north of
the Tweed, such as *fashed* (*fâché*), *ashet* (*assiette*),
and *jigot* (*gigot*), are no less than pure French.
In the times of earliest Scottish poetry, however,
the influence of France had hardly begun to
affect Scottish speech, and in that poetry,
accordingly, a monument is preserved of the
Scottish language in something like its native
state. It would be impossible to render into
modern English of equal simplicity and strength
many of the most ordinary passages in this old
poetry, and for this reason some regret might
be expressed that, at anyrate in Scotland, the
study of poems like Barbour's *Bruce* and
Henry's *Wallace* is abandoned so completely
for the study of early middle-English models.
About the verse of the early Scottish poets
there is a bloom whose secret has vanished
irrevocably with the freshness of their morning-
time ; but from a study of that verse modern
English might at least be enriched with many
beautiful words at present without even a
counterpart in the language.

No fewer than four distinct races were united in the making of the Scottish nation—the original Picts of the north, the Cymry of Strathclyde, the Scots from Ireland, and the Angles of Northumbria. To these might be added a slight later infusion of Norman blood from the south, and the descendants of the sea-roving Norse and Danes who for centuries built their eyries on the coast and among the western isles. So late as the present day the physical characteristics of each of these separate races are observable everywhere with more or less distinctness in the people of the country. With as much truth, though perhaps more subtly, may the mental characteristics of the different races be distinguished. The fact is marked in Sir Walter Scott's famous saying: "Gentlemen of the north, people of the west, men of the south, and folk of Fife." Pains have been taken by more than one critic to identify the respective qualities of these races in the national poetry. Without going so far, it is possible perhaps to trace thus the origin of one or two of the most salient features of the poetry of the north.

To the Celtic element in the Scottish blood Mr. Stopford Brooke attributes the passionate love of wild nature and the love of colour which everywhere distinguish early Scottish from early English poetry. "There is," he says,

speaking of the special Celtic elements in
the Lowland verse, " a passionate, close, and
poetical observation and description of natural
scenery in Scotland from the earliest times of its
poetry such as we do not possess in English
poetry till the time of Wordsworth," while " all
early Scottish poetry differs from English in the
extraordinary way in which colour is insisted
upon, and at times in the lavish exaggeration
of it." The critic's truth in attributing these
characteristics may be easily allowed when it is
remembered how largely to the present hour
colour tinges the nomenclature of the Highlands,
and how full of tenderness for glen and stream
the Highlander still remains. The same delight
in colour may be seen in such passages of
the early *Sir Tristrem* as the description of
Ysonde :

> Ysonde of highe priis,
>   The maiden bright of hewe
> That wered fow and griis
>   And scarlet that was newe.

The same tenderness for wild nature may be
remarked in delicate descriptive passages like
the opening of a certain scene of *The Bruce :*

> This wes in ver, quhen wynter tid,
> With his blastis hidwyss to bid,
> Was our drywyn : and birdis smale,
> As turturis and the nychtyngale,
> Begouth rycht sariely to syng,
> And for to mak in thair singyng

Swete notis and sownys ser
And melodys plesand to her,
And the treis beguth to ma
Burgeans and brycht blomys alsua.

Equally, perhaps, to the Cymric blood may be traced the enthusiasm of nationality which everywhere inspires the poetry of the north. The emigrant Highlander at the present day pines for the "white shieling," and the "yellow island," the "blue mountains," and the "nut-brown maid" he has forsaken ; but no less does the modern farmer of the Clyde valley and the Lanark moors waken to a lively energy at mention of Wallace and the wars with the English. It was in the west that independence always was first asserted, alike in the times of Wallace, of Bruce, and of the later Covenanters ; and in the light of this fact it seems fair to attribute something at least of the strenuous nationality of Scottish poetry, from Barbour's *Bruce* to Burns' *Scots wha hae*, to the strain of British blood in the race.

It cannot be supposed that in the poems which remain to us we possess the very earliest efforts of the Scottish muse. Song is the first of all the arts to make its appearance, and in the two hundred years from the time when Malcolm Canmore, marrying a Saxon wife, began to discourage Celtic as the language of his court, till the time of Thomas the Rhymer, it is not likely that minstrelsy was mute in

the country. Allusions indeed are not lacking
which show that the reading or hearing of
romances was at an early time a popular
relaxation in Scotland ; and there appears to
be reason for believing, as Dr. Irving in his
History of Scottish Poetry suggested, that
the earliest authentic Scottish poem, the *Sir
Tristrem* of Thomas the Rhymer, was one of a
cycle of romances upon the adventures of
ancient, half-mythical Cymric heroes which
formed the popular north-country poetry until
the newly-welded Scottish race came, in
Wallace, Bruce, and Douglas, to possess
national heroes more particularly its own.
Whether or not this be the case, it may be
pointed out that in Scottish poetry there exists,
complete and unbroken from very early times, a
golden vein of historic material. From iron
facts—from the deeds of kings, the fortunes of
war, the loss and gain of provinces—the
historian of Scotland may limn upon his canvas
the outer features of the nation's past. For his
subtler purposes there remains this more delicate
resource. Poetry in Scotland has ever been, not
only a criticism, but a reflection of life, and a
reflection which, like that in the Arabian mirror,
has shown not alone the deeds and manners of
its time, but the thoughts behind the deeds.

Like one of Scotland's own mountain streams
the course of Scottish poetry can be traversed

almost in a day's journey, and at every turn it is seen to have taken its character from its surroundings. From its earliest traces in romance recited to the knights errant of a heroic age, rushing bold and strong down rough defiles in the national war-epics of Barbour and Blind Harry, it is found sunning itself presently in the love-song of James through a primrose strath of peace. At each descent the passion which inspires the verse was the spirit of its age. The wandering knights who after the Conquest pushed their fortunes into the north saw their ideals mirrored in the adventures of a hero like Sir Tristrem. The people new-welded into a single nation by the wars of succession, and battling still against heavy odds for freedom, heard their aspirations echoed in the verse of the chronicler-poets. And the sweet lay penned by the Scottish king heralded the incoming of a gentler time.

Alike as the illustration of a beautiful and heroic old language, as a richly-sparkling fountain of emotion, eloquence, and enthusiasm, and as a reflection, in bright, unfading colours, of the national mind and manners of the north in times that have passed away, the early poetry of Scotland holds a place and character peculiarly its own in the gallery of English literature.

THOMAS THE RHYMER.

THOMAS THE RHYMER.

ON the shadowy borderland between myth and reality, in the early literary history of Scotland, stands The Rhymer, Thomas of Ercildoune. Few names are more familiar than his in the folk-lore of the north, yet regarding few is so little generally known. With his fame as a maker of early Scottish romance a weird reputation for prophecy has been handed down by tradition, while in the ancient ballad poetry of the Borders he is celebrated as the hero of elfin adventure. In this respect he stands on the same platform as Michael Scott and Merlin the Wild, with the latter of whom he has sometimes been confounded; and in the three cases it is curious to note how the superstition of a rude age has, with or without their own connivance, invested the poet and the religious ascetic with the gift of prophecy, and the student of nature with the powers of the wizard.

Of the actual facts of the Rhymer's life very little is known. His name itself even has been subject of speculation. Scott in his introduction to *Sir Tristrem* stated that according to uniform popular

tradition the poet's surname was Learmont, and
that the appellation of 'The Rhymer' was conferred
on him in consequence of his poetical compositions.
But the same writer also remarks that surnames
were not yet always hereditary in the 13th century.
It has never been disputed, however, that the
residence and probable birthplace of the bard was
Ercildoune, now Earlston, a village on the Leader
Water two miles above its junction with the Tweed.
After the lapse of eight centuries a ruined tower
known as his dwelling-place may still be seen at
the western extremity of the village. In a deed of the
thirteenth century by Peter de Haga de Bemersyde,
in the chartulary of Melrose, the Rhymer appears as
a witness; and a charter is extant in the Advocates'
Library at Edinburgh by which Thomas of Ercildoune,
"son and heir of Thomas Rymour of Ercildoune,"
conveys his family lands to the Church of the Holy
Trinity of Soltra. The latter deed is dated 1299,
and from the two charters, and a reference by Henry
the Minstrel, the poet's life may be roughly estimated
as extending from about 1220 to 1298.

Whether he himself explicitly assumed the character
of seer in order to give greater weight to his political
advice is impossible to say. Jamieson, in his *Popular
Ballads*, suggested that, "in order to give a sanction
to his predictions, which seem all to have been
calculated in one way or other for the service of his
country, the Rhymer pretended to an intercourse
with the Queen of Elfland, as Numa Pompilius did
with the nymph Egeria." This may have been the

case, or the story may be altogether a popular and later invention ; but the narrative of his intercourse with the elfin queen, whether composed by himself or not, is extant to the present day, and forms one of the most characteristic of the Border ballads. According to this ballad, Thomas sojourned with the queen in Elfland for seven years, though to him it seemed " nought but the space of dayis three." At parting, by way of consolation, she revealed to her sorrowing lover a long roll of prophecies, and as a farewell token conferred on Thomas himself the prophetic gift :

> If thou wilt spell or talès tell,
> Thomas, thou never shall make lee.

With a story of this sort once established in the popular mind it is easy to see how the Rhymer might acquire the reputation of a prophet. There exists, as has been said, no absolute proof that he assumed the prophetic *rôle* himself, but it is certain that very shortly after his death the foresight of many momentous events was attributed to him. The most striking of these perhaps is that of the accidental death of Alexander III. at Kinghorn, and the subsequent disastrous wars of succession. The story is related both by Fordun and Boece. The latter, translated by Bellenden, gives it with no small dramatic skill. " It is said the day afore the kingis deith the Erle of Marche demandit ane prophet namit Thomas Rymour, otherwayis namit Ersiltoun, quhat wedder suld be on the morow. To quhome answerit this Thomas that on the morow, afore noun, sall blow the gretist wynd that ever was hard afore in Scotland. On the morow, quhen it was neir noun, the lift appering loune, but (without) ony din or tempest, the Erle send for this propheit and reprevit hym that he prognosticat sic wynd to be, and nae apperance thairof. This Thomas maid litel answer, bot said, noun is not yet gane. And incontinent ane man came to the yet (gate) schawing the king was slane. Than said the prophet, yone is the wynd that sall blaw to the gret calamity and truble of al Scotland." Prophecies attributed to the Rhymer are recorded by Barbour, Wyntoun, and Blind Harry, and are mentioned in the *Scala-chronicon*, a history written, it is supposed, in the time of Edward III. Bits of local prophecy quoted as his were floating in the popular mind so late as the beginning of the present century, and may indeed remain in currency to the present day. One of these is pathetic enough:

> The hare sall kittle (litter) on my hearth stane,
> And there will never be a laird Learmont again.

Most of the extant political rhymes passing as the prophecies of True Thomas are to be found, with other productions of the same sort, in a small volume published by Andro Hart at Edinburgh in 1615.

Behind all this popular tradition of elfin intercourse and prophetic insight, however, Thomas the Rhymer claims the solid reputation of maker of the earliest Scottish romance. There exist two other compositions of competing claim—the romances of *Gawen and*

Gologras and *Galoran of Galloway* — both also attributed by Scott to the thirteenth century. Strong doubts as to their date, however, have been expressed by later critics, while their rudeness and excessive alliteration render them hardly intelligible. *Sir Tristrem* therefore may fairly be looked upon, not only as the most outstanding, but as the earliest extant poem of the north.

The poem is contained in the famous Auchinleck manuscript, "a portly quarto volume of early English poetry written on vellum in the beginning of the fourteenth century," and presented to the Advocates' Library in 1744 by Lord Auchinleck, father of Boswell, the biographer of Johnson. The former history of the volume is unknown. From this source *Sir Tristrem* was very fully edited by Scott in 1804, and in 1886 was made still further accessible in an admirable edition for the Scottish Text Society by Mr. G. P. M'Neill.

It is true of this, of course, as of most other productions of obscure times, that the authorship has been subjected to question. The point upon which doubt has been chiefly urged is the opening stanza of the romance:

> Y was at Ertheldoune
> With Tomas spak Y thare, &c.

It may be possible to make too much of this point. The insertion of his name in the text was in early times a poet's only method of perpetuating his claims of authorship. After detailing all that has been said for and against the authenticity of the romance, Mr. M'Neill quotes the direct testimony of the Rhymer's contemporary, Robert Mannyng of Brunne, and concludes by remarking that "the arguments which assail the trustworthiness of these documents are suggested by somewhat hypercritical doubts, and the theories designed to supplant them are based upon conjectures wholly unsupported by evidence."

The invention of the story told in the poem, however, cannot be attributed to the Rhymer. The tale of Tristrem most probably had a foundation in the exploits of an actual chieftain of the ancient Cymric kingdom of western Britain. In the early Welsh Triads Tristrem appears, already famous, chiefly as the lover of Essylt, wife of his uncle Mark. In the history of King Arthur, compiled by Geoffrey of Monmouth in the ninth century, the hero is recorded as one of the knights of the Round Table. Frequent mention of the story of Tristrem and Isolde is found in the twelfth and thirteenth century songs of the troubadours and trouveres of France; and it formed one of the four great romances of Cymric tradition recited at the court of the Anglo-Norman kings. It is for casting the romance into Scottish verse that credit is given to the Rhymer; and his composition soon became known throughout Europe as the best version of the famous tale. Robert of Brunne declared—

> Ouer gestes it has the steem,
> Ouer all that is or was,
> If men it sayd as made Thomas.

After wanderings down the centuries in almost every tongue of Europe, the story is found living yet in modern days in the verse of Richard Wagner, Matthew Arnold, Lord Tennyson, and Mr. Swinburne.

As it remains, the early Scottish composition is a vivid example, as indeed it was perhaps the most famous model, of the romances of chivalry. Already the story had lost the primitive simplicity of legend and had had incorporated with it all the mediæval devices of plot and motive. Love and arms are the subjects—the rescue of usurped kingdoms and the prosecution of amorous intrigues. To these ends giants and dragons have to be overcome and a love-potion has to be drunk. These were the regular machinery of the singers of Europe in the Middle Ages. The chief thread of the narrative bears that the British knight Tristrem is sent to bring home from Ireland his uncle's bride Isonde, and by the mistaken drinking of a love-philtre by the two on the way, becomes engaged in an amour which occupies the remainder of the lovers' lives. Strata- gems, estrangements, stolen interviews follow, a very doubtful regard is paid to conjugal relations, and the whole tale forms material for somewhat curious speculation upon the morals and habits of a society which had these romances for its approved intellectual food.

The poem is written in an involved stanza in striking contrast to the simple style of the narrative and the obvious eagerness of the narrator to press on with his tale. The design of the composition, as in most old romances, is of the character best adapted for recitation—a series of adventures, each complete in itself, strung upon the lives of the lovers. At the same time there is a certain arrangement, a proportion and balance of parts round the central idea, which give to the story an artistic unity. The situations frequently possess strong dramatic point, as when Tristrem, having drunk the love-potion with Isonde, has to fulfil his mission and hand her over in marriage to the king. Most notable of all, the characters of the tale from first to last are firmly and even subtly drawn. Limned from the outside by their actions and words, they stand distinct as if reproduced from life or from the most intimate tradition. Reliably as in actual contact one comes to know them all—Isonde, another Lady Macbeth, crafty of brain and passionate of heart; "Brengwain the Bright," the maid and confidant of the queen, careful by the possession of compromising secrets to keep Isonde in her power, but at the same time both lending her wits and submitting her person to screen her mistress; Mark, the rich king and foolish husband, tricked and deceived, yielding up his queen, Herod-like, for a minstrel's song, and ever ready to believe a protestation in face of the clearest evidence; and Tristrem, the doughty knight, skilled alike in arts and arms, fertile in amorous devices, and faithful everywhere to the lady of his passion. Even the subordinate characters are touched to the life. A modern analytic poet might be glad to own a delicate bit of motive-painting like the scene in

which Sir Canados woos Isonde and receives his
answer.

The example of Sir Tristrem had some following
in Scottish poetry. To the Rhymer himself Scott
was inclined to attribute *Hornchild, or The Geste of
King Horn*, a romantic narrative poem extant in six-
syllable couplets. There exist also the two alliterative
Arthurian romances before-mentioned of *Gawen and
Gologras* and *Galoran of Galloway; The Pystyl of
Swete Susan*, a poem in involved stanza like that of
Sir Tristrem, but of longer line, on the Apocryphal
subject of Susanna; and *The Taill of Rauf Coilzear,
how he harbreit King Charles*, a vigorous romance
concerning Charlemagne and Ralph a collier, similar
in incident to the story of King Alfred and the
shepherd. But another inspiration was already
in the air. Shortly after the composition of *Sir
Tristrem* the last of the line of Celtic kings fell
over the fatal cliff at Kinghorn, and amid the dire
wars of succession and independence a new era
dawned upon the history and literature of Scotland.

THE selections from *Sir Tristrem* which are here given include the most salient episodes of the romance. No liberties have been taken with the text, saving the insertion of capitals for the first personal pronoun and at proper names. The ancient spelling, *yiue* (give), *yuere* (ivere, ivory), *tviis* (twice), possesses a historic interest of its own. The chief peculiarity of the composition is its elliptic style :

> That man hye neuer seighe
> That bifor Tristrem wold,

is left to stand for

> That man she never saw
> That before Tristrem she would choose.

Notwithstanding this obstacle it is curious to discover how clearly the meaning appears when the stanzas are read aloud. Phonetically the language differs but little from modern English.

SIR TRISTREM.

 WAS at Ertheldoune:
　　With Tomas spak Y thare;
　　Ther herd Y rede in roune[1]
Who Tristrem gat and bare,
Who was king with croun,
　　And who him forsterd yare[2],
And who was bold baroun,
　　As thair elders ware.
　　　　Bi yere[3]
　　Tomas tells in toun
This auentours[4] as thai ware.

The Birth of Tristrem.

[Truce having been declared between two chiefs, the Duke Morgan and Rouland Riis, Lord of Ermonie, the latter betakes himself to the court of King Mark. Victorious at a tournament, he becomes the object of a passion on the part of the king's sister, Blancheflour, who, the knight presently being wounded, visits him secretly in his chamber. Word, however, arrives from Rohand, a trusty vassal, that Morgan has broken the truce. Rouland therefore, followed by Blancheflour, takes leave of Mark.]

　　Thai busked and maked hem boun[5],
　　　　Nas ther no leng abade;

1 raised ensign.

Thai lefted goinfainoun[1],
   And out of hauen thai rade
Till thai com til atoun,
   A castel Rohand had made.
Her sailes thai leten doun,
   And knight, ouer bord thai strade
      Al cladde.

2 brave, faithful.

   The knightes that wer fade[2],
Thai dede as Rohand bade.

Rohand right he radde:—
   "This maiden schal ben oure,
Rouland Riis to wedde,

3 to rule.

   At weld[3] in castel tour,
To bring hir to his bedde
   That brightest is in bour.

4 nourished.

Nas neuer non fairer fedde[4]
   Than Maiden Blauncheflour
      Al blithe."

5 much honour.
6 swiftly.

   After that michel anour[5]
Parting com ther swithe[6].

7 in public it was not hidden.

In hird nas nought to hele[7]
   That Morgan telles in toun,

8 amiably (meekly) 'gan mix.
9 speak.

Mekeliche he gan mele[8]
   Among his men to roun[9];
He bad his knightes lele

10 summons.

   Come to his somoun[10]

With hors and wepenes fele
  And rered goinfaynoun,
      That bold.
  He rode so king with croun
  To win al that he wold.

Of folk the feld was brade,
  Ther Morgan men gan bide[1];
Tho Rouland to hem rade,
  Oyain him gun thai ride;
Swiche meting nas neuer made
  With sorwe on ich aside.
Ther of was Rouland glade,
  Ful fast he feld[2] her pride.
      With paine
  Morgan scaped that tide
  That he nas nought slain.

Morganes folk cam newe[3]
  Of Rouland Riis the gode,
On helmes gun thai hewe,
  Thurch brinies brast[4] the blod;
Sone to deth ther drewe
  Mani a frely fode[5].
Of Rouland was to rewe[6],
  To grounde when he yode[7],
      That bold:
  His sone him after stode,
  And dere his deth he sold.

Rewthe mow[8] ye here
  Of Rouland Riis the knight:

[1] abide, take up position.

[2] felled.

[3] came anew upon.

[4] through helmet burst.

[5] noble person.

[6] rue.

[7] go-ed, went.

[8] sorrow must.

Threhundred he slough there
  With his swerd bright;
Of all tho that ther were
  Might none him felle in fight,
But on with tresoun there
  Thurch the bodi him pight[1].
     With gile
  To deth he him dight—
Allas that ich while!

His hors o feld him bare
  Alle ded hom in his way;
Gret wonder hadde he thought thare
  That folk of ferly play[2].
The tiding com with care
  To Blauncheflour, that may[3].
For hir me reweth sare:
  On child bed ther sche lay
     Was born
  Of hir Tristrem that day,
Ac hye no bade[4] nought that morn.

A ring of rich hewe
  Than hadde that leuedi fre[5];
Sche toke it Rouhand trewe,
  Hir sone sche bad it be:—
"Mi brother wele it knewe,
  Mi fader yaf[6] it me;

[1] pierced.

[2] Great wonder had he gained by his marvellous activity.

[3] damsel.

[4] But she lingered not.

[5] noble lady.

[6] gave.

King Markes may rewe,
  The ring, than he it se,
      And moun.
As Rouland loued the,
Thou kepe it to his sone."

The folk stode vnfain[1]
  Bifor that leuedi fre:—
"Rouland, mi lord, is slain,
  He speketh no more with me.
That leuedi, nought to lain[2],
  For sothe[3] ded is sche.
Who may be ogain?
  As God wil it schal be,
      Vnblithe."
  Sorwe it was to se,
That leuedi swelted swithe[4].

Geten and born was so
  The child, was fair and white.
Nas neuer Rohand so wo,
  He nist[5] it whom to wite[6].
To child bed ded he go
  His owhen wiif al so tite[7],
And seyd he hadde children to,
  On hem was his delite
      Bi crist.
  In court men cleped[8] him so:—
Tho tram bifor the trist.

[1] sad.

[2] not to dispute, without a doubt.
[3] forsooth.

[4] died soon.

[5] wist not.
[6] to blame, to put it upon.

[7] quickly.

[8] called.

Tristrem at the Court of Mark.

[For fifteen years Tristrem, disguised as Tramtrist, is educated by Rohand, becoming marvellously expert in all knightly games, in minstrelsy, and hunting. At last, one day, Tristrem having won heavily at chess from the master of a Norwegian vessel, the latter, to avoid payment, carries his opponent off. A heavy storm constraining the master of the vessel to put him ashore, Jonahlike, in England, Tristrem makes his way by chance to the court of Mark, and there, by his skill in music and venery, becomes a favourite of the king. Meanwhile Rohand, searching through seven kingdoms for his foster-son, arrives at last at the palace gate. On account of his tattered and travel-stained clothes he is refused entrance, first by the porter, then by the usher.]

The pouer man of mold
 Tok forth another ring,
The huscher he yaf the gold,
 It seemed to a king;
Formest tho in fold[1]
 He lete him in thring[2];
To Tristrem trewe in hold
 He hete[3] he wold him bring,
    And brought;
 Tristrem knewe him no thing,
And ferly[4] Rohand thought.

Thei men Tristrem had sworn,
 He no trowed[5] it neuer in lede[6]
That Rohand robes were torn,
 That he wered swiche awede[7].
He frained[8] him biforn[9]:—
 "Child, so God the rede[10],

[1] Foremost then among the folk.
[2] press in.
[3] promised.
strangely.
[5] believed.
[6] indeed (*lit.* among the people).
[7] wore such a dress.
[8] asked.
[9] before, first.
[10] judge.

How were thou fram Rohand lorn[1]?
  Monestow neuer[2] in lede?"
      Nought lain
  He kneled better spede
And kist Rohand ful fain.

[1] lost.

[2] Rememberest thou never.

"Fader, no wretthe the nought[3],
  Ful welcome er ye!
Bi God, that man hath bought,
  No thing no knewe Y the;
With sorwe thou hast me sought,
  To wite it wo is me!"
To Mark the word he brought,
  "Wil ye mi fader se
      With sight?
  Graithed[4] Y wil he be,
And seththen[5] schewe him as knight."

[3] be not wrathful.

[4] clad.

[5] afterwards (*mod. Scot.* syne).

Tristrem to Mark it seyd,
  His auentours, as it were,
Hou he with schipmen pleyd,
  Of lond hou thai him bere,
Hou stormes hem bi stayed,
  Til anker hem brast and are[6].
"Thai yolden[7] me that Y layd
  With al mi wining there
      In hand;
  Y clambe the holtes hare[8]
Till Y thine hunters fand."

[6] anchor and oar broke.

[7] yielded.

[8] woods hoar.

A bath thai brought Rohand inne,
A barbour was redi thare;
Al rowe[1] it was, his chinne,
His heued[2] was white of hare;
A scarlet with riche skinne[3]
Ybrought him was ful yare.
Rohand of noble kinne,
That robe ful fair he bare,
That bold;
Who that had seyn him thare
A prince him might han told.

Fair his tale bi gan
Rohand; thei he com lat[4];
Tristrem, that honour can,
To halle led him the gate[5].
Ich man seyd than
Nas non swiche, as thai wate[6],
As was the pouer man
That thai bete fram the gat
With care;
Nas non that wald him hate,
Bot welcom was he thare.

Water thai asked swithe,
Cloth and board was drain[7]
With mete and drink lithe[8]
And seriaunce[9] that were bayn[10]
To serve Tristrem swithe
And Sir Rohand ful fayn;

[1] rough.
[2] head.
[3] a scarlet robe fur-lined.
[4] thither he let him come.
[5] way.
[6] knew.
[7] drawn.
[8] pleasant.
[9] servants.
[10] ready.

Whasche[1], when thai wald rise,
  The king ros him oyain
    That tide ;
In lede is nought to layn[2],
He sett him bi his side.

Rohand that was thare,
  To Mark his tale bi gan :—
"Wist ye what Tristrem ware,
  Miche gode ye wold him an[3].
Your owhen soster him bare,"
  —The king lithed[4] him than—
"Y nam sibbe[5] him na mare,
  Ich aught[6] to ben his man,
    Sir king.
  Knowe it yiue[7] ye can,
Sche taught[8] me this ring

When Rouland Riis the bold
  Douke Morgan gan mete."
The tale when Rohand told,
  For sorwe he gan grete[9].
The king biheld that old,
  How his wonges[10] were wete.
To Mark the ring he yold,
  He knewe it al so sket[11],
    Gan loke :
  He kist Tristrem ful skete,
And for his nevou[12] toke.

[1] wash.

[2] in company is not to be disputed, to be brief.

[3] grant.

[4] listened to.

[5] kin to.

[6] owned.

[7] gif, if.

[8] entrusted to.

[9] weep.

[10] cheeks.

[11] quickly.

[12] nephew.

[1] then they kissed.

Tho thai kisten[1] him alle,
    Bothe leuedi and knight
And seriaunce in the halle
    And maidens that were bright.
Tristrem gan Rohand calle,

[2] asked.

    And freined[2] him with sight :—
" Sir, how may this falle?
    How may Y proue it right?

[3] in short.

        Nought lain[3]
Tel me, for Godes might,
    How was mi fader slain?"

Tristrem's Revenge.

[Told of the death of his father and mother by Morgan's treachery, Tristrem at last obtains Mark's permission to make war. He is knighted by the king, and, sailing for Ermonie, garrisons Rohand's castle with a thousand men. Grown weary there of inaction, he determines to put his fortune to a personal issue.]

" With Morgan speke wil Y
        And spede.
So long idel we ly,
    Myself mai do mi nede."

[4] promised.
[5] ready.
[6] His fifteen knights.
[7] gaed, went.

[8] sheared, cut.

Tristrem dede as he hight[4].
    He busked and made him yare[5]
Hi fiftend som of knight[6],
    With him yede[7] na mare.
To court thai com ful right
    As Morgan his brede schare[8];

Thai teld tho bi sight
  Ten kinges sones thai ware;
    Vn sought
  Heuedes of wild bare
Ichon[1] to presant brought.

             1 each one.

Rohand bi gan to sayn[2],
  To his knightes than seyd he :—
"As woman is, tviis for lain[3],
  Y may say bi me.
Yif Tristrem be now sleyn,
  Yuel yemers[4] er we.
To armes, knight and swayn,
  And swiftly ride ye
    And swithe!
  Till Y Tristrem se,
No worth[5] Y neuer blithe."

             2 speak.

             3 As a woman who is twice seduced.

             4 ill guardians.

             5 become.

Tristrem speke bi gan :—
  "Sir King, God loke[6] the
As Y the loue and an[7]
  And thou hast serued to me !"
The Douke answerd than :—
  "Y pray, mi lord so fre,
Whether thou bless or ban,
  Thine owhen mot it be,
    Thou bold !
  Thi nedes tel thou me,
Thine erand, what thou wold."

             6 look on.
             7 regard.

"Amendes! Mi fader is slain,
　　Mine hirritage Hermonie!"
The Douk answerd ogain :—
　　"Certes, thi fader than slough Y.
Seththen[1] thou so hast sayd,
　　Amendes ther ought to ly.
Ther fore, prout swayn,
　　So schal Y the; for thi
　　　　Right than
　　Artow comen titly[2]
Fram Marke thi kinsman.

"Yongling, thou schalt abide!
　　Foles thou wendest to fand[3]!
Thi fader thi moder gan hide,
　　In horedom he hir band[4].
How comestow with pride?
　　Out, traitour, of mi land!"
Tristrem spac that tide :—
　　"Thou lext[5], ich vnder stand
　　　　And wot[6]!"
　　Morgan with his hand
With a lof Tristrem smot.

On his brest adoun
　　Of his nose ran the blod.
Tristrem swerd was boun,
　　And near the Douke he stode.*
　　*　　*　　*　　*　　*

　　　*　　*　　*　　*　　*

* Two lines are here wanting, as is evident from the difference
in the stanza, though there is no blank in the MS.

[1] syne, there-
　　after.

[2] Thou art come
　　quickly.

[3] weenedst to
　　find.

[4] bound.

[5] liest.

[6] know.

With that, was comen to toun
  Rohand with help ful gode
      And gayn[1].
  Al that oyain[2] hem stode
Wightly[3] were thai slayn.

1 pleasant.
2 against.
3 quickly.

To prisoun thai gun take
  Erl, baroun, and knight.
For Douke . Morgan sake,
  Mani on dyd doun right.
Schaftes they gun shake
  And riuen scheldes bright
Crounes thai gun crake
  Mani, ich wene, aplight[4].
      Saunfayl[5],
  Bitvene the none and the night
Last the batayle.

4 outright.
5 without pause.

Thus hath Tristrem the swete
  Yslawe the Douke Morgan.
No wold he neuer lete[6]
  Til mo castels were tan[7];
Tounes thai yold him skete,
  And cites stithe of stan[8].
The folk fel to his fet,
  Ayaines him stode ther nan
      In land.
  He slough his fader ban,[9]
Al bowed to his hand.

6 forbear.
7 ta'en.
8 strong of stone.
9 father's
  murderer.

1 ruled.

Tvo yere he sett[1] that land,
His lawes made he cri.
Al com to his hand,
Almain, and Ermonie,
At his wil to stand
Boun and al redy.

2 gave.

Rohand he yaf[2] the wand,
And bad him sitt him bi,

3 noble.

That fre[3].
" Rohand lord make Y,
To held this lond of me."

Tristrem's Teaching of Ysonde.

[Returned to his uncle's court, Tristrem finds the country
groaning under a huge, unjust tribute demanded by Ireland—
three hundred pounds each of gold, coined silver, and brass, and
every fourth year three hundred children. Tristrem persuades
the council to refuse, takes upon himself the denial of the tribute,
and in a great duel with Moraunt, the Irish ambassador, cleaves
that champion's skull. At the same time he is himself wounded,
and the wound gangrenes. He lies ill for three years. At last,
despairing of cure and forsaken by all because of his wound's
stench, he asks a ship. In this he drifts from Carlion to Dublin.
There his skill in music, chess, and tables enlists the interest of
the queen, who, expert in surgery, after the manner of the ladies
of that day, undertakes his cure. The queen is sister to the
dead Moraunt, but, remembering his duel, Tristrem has taken
care to assume the name of Tramtris, and to declare himself a
merchant robbed by pirates. As an accomplished companion he
is frequently invited to court, and there he turns his skill to
good account.]

4 was called.

The king had a douhter dere
That maiden Ysonde hight[4],

5 song.
6 lief, pleased.

That gle[5] was lef[6] to here
And romaunce to rede aright.

7 teach.

Sir Tramtris hir gan lere[7]

Tho with al his might
What alle pointes[1] were,
  To se the sothe[2] in sight,
     To say.
In Yrlond nas no knight
With Ysonde durst play.

Ysonde of heighe priis[3],
  The maiden bright of hewe
That wered fow and griis[4]
  And scarlet that was newe.
In warld was non so wiis
  Of craft that men knewe
With outen Sir Tramtris,
  That al games of grewe
     On grounde.
Hom longeth[5] Tramtris the trewe,
For heled was his wounde.

Sir Tramtris in Irlond
  Duelled al ayere.
So gode likeing[6] he fand
  That hole he was and fere.
The Quen to fot and hand
  He serued dern and dere[7];
Ysonde he dede vnder stand
  What alle playes were
     In lay[8].
His leue he asked at here
In schip to founde[9] oway.

[1] accomplishments.
[2] truth.
[3] praise, fame.
[4] fur and grey furred cloth.
[5] entertains with fair talk.
[6] entertainment.
[7] secretly and with favour.
[8] law.
[9] go.

The Embassy for Ysonde.

[Returned to the court of Mark, Tristrem is received with
great joy by his uncle, and has to give a full account of his
absence and cure. He dilates upon the charms of Ysonde, and
the king, struck by the description, offers to make Tristrem his
heir if he will bring the princess to Cornwall. The idea pleases
the jealous barons.]

In Inglond ful wide
   The barouns hem bi thought
To fel Tristremes pride
   How thai fairest mought;
The king thai rad to ride[1],
   A quen to him thai sought,
That Tristrem might abide[2]
   That he no were[3] it nought,
     No king:
Thai seyd that Tristrem mought
Ysonde of Irlond bring.

A brid bright thai ches[4]
   As blod opon snoweing:
" A maiden of swiche reles[5],
   Tristrem may to the bring."
Quoth Tristrem :—'" It is les[6],
   And troweth it for lesing[7];
To aski that neuer no wes,
   It is a fole[8] askeing
     Bi kinde;
It is a selli[9] thing,
For no man may it finde.

[1] counselled to rid himself of (Tristrem).

[2] suffer.

[3] become.

[4] chose.

[5] of such sort.

[6] lies.

[7] leasing, treason.

[8] foolish.

[9] strange, silly.

" Y rede[1] ye nought no striue ;　　　　　[1] counsel.

　A swalu Ich herd sing,

Ye sigge Ich wern mi nem to wiue[2],　　　[2] Ye say I dare
　　　　　　　　　　　　　　　　　　　　　my uncle to
　For Y schuld be your king.　　　　　　　wed.

Now bringeth me atte riue[3]　　　　　　　[3] (*à la rive*)shore.

　Schip and other thing.

Ye se me neuer oliue[4]　　　　　　　　　　[4] Ye will never
　　　　　　　　　　　　　　　　　　　　　　see me alive.
　Bot yif Ich Ysonde bring,

　　That bright.

Finde me min askeing,

Mine fiftend som of knight."

The Drinking of the Love-potion.

[Tristrem sails for Ireland with rich presents, to find the
people of Dublin in dire terror. They are threatened by a
monstrous dragon which has done so much damage that the
hand of Ysonde is offered to him who shall slay it. Tristrem
undertakes the adventure, and after a dreadful encounter slays
the beast. Cutting out the dragon's tongue he attempts to
carry it away in his hose, but is overcome by its poison.
Presently the king's steward, passing, cuts off the dragon's head,
carries it to court, and claims the victory and the hand of Ysonde.
The princess disbelieves the tale, and proceeding with her
mother to the scene of encounter, finds Tristrem. Revived by
their aid, he claims the victory, proves his claim by producing
the tongue, and pledges his ship and cargo that he will make
good his story upon the person of the steward. So dignified is
the supposed merchant's bearing that Ysonde exclaims " Alas
that thou art not knight !" While Tristrem is in a bath Ysonde
discovers that a break in his sword fits a fragment of steel which
had been taken from the skull of her uncle Moraunt. With her
mother she rushes to despatch the champion in his bath, but the
king interposes. Tristrem defends himself as having slain
Moraunt in fair fight. Smiling upon Ysonde, he tells her that
he is her late preceptor Tramtris, and asks her why she did not
slay him when she had opportunity before. Finally he declares
his embassy. The match is accepted, the steward relinquishing
his claim, is thrown into prison at Ysonde's request, and
preparation is made for the voyage of the princess.

Tristrem swore that thing;
   Thai seyd it schuld stand
That he schuld Ysonde bring
   —Thai token it vnder hand—
To Marke, the riche king,
   Oliue yif thai him fand,
And make hir with his ring,
   Quen of Ingeland,
        To say;
   The forward[1] fast thai band[2]
Er thai parted oway.

No asked he lond no lithe[3],
   Bot that maiden bright;
He busked him al so swithe[4],
   Both squier and knight.
Her moder about was blithe
   And tok adrink of might,
That loue wald kithe[5],
   And tok it Brengwain the bright
        To think:
   "At er spouscing a night
Yif Mark and hir to drink."

Ysonde bright of hewe
   Is fer out in the se.
A winde oyain hem blewe
   That sail no might ther be.
So rewe[6] the knightes trewe,
   Tristrem, so rewe he,
Euer as thai com newe—

[1] compact.
[2] bound.

[3] neither land nor people.

[4] speedily.

[5] beget.

[6] rowed.

He on oyain hem thre[1]—
> Gret swink[2].
Swete Ysonde the fre
Asked Bringwain adrink.

The coupe was richeli wrought,
> Of gold it was, the pin *;
In al the warld nas nought
> Swiche drink as ther was in.
Brengwain was wrong bi thought,
> To that drink sche gan win
And swete Ysonde it bi taught[3];
> Sche bad Tristrem bigin,
> > To say.
> Her loue might no man tvin[4],
Til her endingday.

An hounde ther was biside,
> That was yclepcd Hodain;
The coupe he licked that tide
> Tho doun it sett Bringwain;
Thai loued al in lide[5]
> And ther of were thai fain;
To gider[6] thai gun abide
> In ioie and ek in pain
> > For thought:
> In iuel time, to sain[7],
The drink was y wrought.

[1] He one against three of them.
[2] toil.
[3] gave.
[4] part.
[5] in common.
[6] Together.
[7] to say, forsooth.

* Scott explained this line by a note: "The practice of putting gold and silver pins into drinking vessels was intended to regulate the draught of each guest." Hence perhaps the vulgar expressions, "drinking to a merry pin," and "taking one down a peg."

1 Two weeks.

Tvai wikes[1] in the strand
  No seyl thai no drewe;
Into Inglond
  A winde to wille hem blewe.
The king on hunting thai fand;
  A knaue that he knewe,
He made him knight with hand
  For his tidinges newe,
      Gan bring.
  Ysonde bright of hewe
Ther spoused Mark the king.

[Brengwain on the nuptial night is substituted for the guilty queen. Presently the latter, fearing betrayal, orders two ruffians to dispatch her maid. The damsel, however, induces these to spare her, protesting that her only crime has been to lend the queen a clean smock on her bridal night. This being reported to the queen as Brengwain's last speech, Ysonde perceives the fidelity of her maid, laments her death, and vows vengeance on her murderers. Brengwain is then produced and restored to full favour.]

Mark surrenders his Queen.

Fram Irlond to .the king
  An harpour com bi tven[2];

2 between, across.

An harp he gan forth bring,
  Swiche no hadde thai neuer sen
      With sight;

3 without pause.

  Himself, with outen wen[3],
Bar it day and night.

Ysonde he loved in are[1],
  He that the harp brought;
About his hals[2] he it bare,
  Richelich it was wrought;
He hidde it euer mare[3],
  Out no com it nought.
"Thine harp whi wiltow spare,
  Yif thou ther of can ought
      Of gle[4]?"
  "Out no cometh it nought
With outen yiftes fre[5]."

Mark seyd, "Lat me se
  Harpi hou thou can,
And what thou askest me
  Yiue Y schal the than."
"Blethely[6]," seyd he;
  A miri lay he bigan.
"Sir king, of yiftes fre
  Her with Ysonde Y wan[7]
      Bidene[8].
  Y proue the for fals man,
Or Y schal haue thi quen."

Mark to conseyl yede[9],
  And asked rede[10] of tho to:
"Lesen Y mote[11] mi manhed,
  Or yeld Ysonde me fro."
Mark was ful of drede,
  Ysonde lete he go.

[1] erst, formerly.

[2] neck.

[3] evermore.

[4] music.

[5] noble gifts.

[6] Blithely.

[7] win.

[8] speedily.

[9] went.

[10] advice.
[11] Lessen I must.

Tristrem in that nede[1]
   At wode was, dere to slo[2],
      That day;
  Tristrem com right tho
As Ysonde was o way.

Tho was Tristrem in ten[3],
  And chidde with the king;
"Yifstow glewemen[4] thy quen?
  Hastow no nother thing?"
His rote[5], with outen wen[6],
  He raught[7] by the ring;
Tho folwed Tristrem the ken
  To schip ther thai hir bring
      So blithe;
  Tristrem bigan to sing,
And Ysonde bigan to lithe[8].

Swiche song he gan sing
  That hir was swithe wo[9];
Her com swiche louelonging,
  Hir hert brast neighe ato[10].
Therl[11] to hir gan spring
  With knightes mani mo,
And seyd, "Mi swete thing,
  Whi farestow so,
      Y pray?"
  Ysonde to lond most go,
Er sche went o way.

1 extremity.

2 slaying deer.

3 anger.

4 Givest thou gleemen.

5 a musical instrument, hand-organ.
6 without delay.
7 reached for.

8 listen.

9 soon sorrowful.

10 nigh broke in two.

11 The earl.

"Within a stounde[1] of the day
  Y schal ben hole and sounde;
Y here amenstrel[2], to say,
  Of Tristrem he hath asoun[3]."
Therl seyd, "Dathet him ay[4]
  Of Tristrem yif this stounde!
That minstrel for his lay
    Schal have an hundred pounde
      Of me,
Yif he wil with ous founde[5],
Lef,[6] for thou louest his gle."

His gle al for to here
  The leuedi was sett on land
To play bi the riuere;
  Therl ladde hir bi hand;
Tristrem, trewe fere[7],
  Mirie notes he fand
Opon his rote of yuere[8],
  As thai were on the strand;
    That stounde
Thurch that semly sand[9]
Ysonde was hole and sounde.

Hole sche was and sounde
  Thurch vertu of his gle;
For thi therl that stounde
  Glad a man was he;
Of penis to hundred pounde
  He yaf[10] Tristrem the fre;

[1] short space.

[2] a minstrel.

[3] a song.

[4] Ill-luck have him always.

[5] go.

[6] Love, darling.

[7] friend.

[8] ivory.

[9] sound.

[10] gave.

To schip than gun thai founde,
In Yrlond wald thai be
Ful fain[1],
Therl and knightes thre
With Ysonde and Bringwain.

Tristrem tok his stede
And lepe ther on to ride;
The quen bad him her lede[2]
To schip him bi side;
Tristrem dede as hye bede[3],
In wode he gan hir hide.
To therl he seyd, "In that nede
Thou hast ytent[4] thi pride,
Thou dote!
With thine harp thou wonne hir that tide,
Thou tint hir with mi rote."

Meriadok's Discovery.

[After a week spent together in the forest Tristrem restores Ysonde to the king, telling him to give minstrels other gifts in future. The suspicions of one of Mark's courtiers, however, have been excited.]

Meriadok was aman
That Tristrem trowed ay[5];
Miche gode he him an,
In o[6] chaumber thai lay.
Tristrem to Ysonde wan[7]
A night with hir to play;

[1] willingly.

[2] lead.

[3] as she bade.

[4] lost.

[5] trusted always.

[6] one.

[7] won.

As man that miche kan[1],
  A bord he tok oway
    Of hei bour *;
Er he went, to say,
Of snowe was fallen aschour.

[1] can do much.

A schowr ther was y falle,
  That al the way was white;
Tristrem was wo with alle,
  With diol, sorwe, and site[2].
Bitven the bour and the halle
  The way was naru and lite[3].
Swiche cas him was bi falle,
  As we finde in scrite[4].
    Ful sket
  A siue[5] he fond tite[6],
And bond vnder his fete.

[2] dule, sorrow, and anxiety. MS. "and sorwe site."
[3] little.
[4] writing.
[5] sieve.
[6] quickly.

Meriadok with his might
  Aros vp al bi dene[7];
The way he went right
  Til he com to the quen;
The bord he fond of tvight[8],
  To wite, and nought at wene[9].
Of Tristrem kertel the knight
  He fond a pece grene
    Of tore;
  Meriadok the kene
Wondred ther fore.

[7] with speed.
[8] twitched off.
[9] To be perceived without doubt (plainly).

* Scott notes here the primitive domestic architecture. The queen's chamber was a wooden bower apart, "the art of partitions being probably unknown."

The Trial of Ysonde.

[Meriadok opens his suspicions to the king. The latter
accordingly pretends a journey to the Holy Land, and asks
Ysonde to whose charge she wishes to be committed. At first
she names Tristrem, but presently, advised by Brengwain, she
pretends a hatred to the knight, and the king is satisfied.
Further interviews of the lovers are discovered by a dwarf,
concealed in a tree. The king assumes the dwarf's place, but
the lovers, discovering him by his shadow, pretend mutual
recrimination, and Mark is again persuaded of their innocence.
Finally, however, Meriadok invents a device. The king, the
queen, and Tristrem have blood let the same day, and Meriadok
strews the floor of Ysonde's chamber with flour. Tristrem
coming at night, leaps thirty feet over the flour, but his vein
bursting betrays his visit.]

Tristrem was fled oway,
　　To wite, and nought to wene.
At Londen on a day
　　Mark wald spourge[1] the quen.
Men seyd sche brak the lay[2];
　　A bischop yede[3] bi tvene,
　　　With hot yren, to say,
　　Sche thought to make hir clenc
　　　　Of sake[4].
　　Ysonde said bidene
That dome sche wald take.

Men sett the merkes[5] there
　　At Westeminster ful right,
Hot yren to bere
　　For Sir Tristrem the knight.
In pouer wede to were[6]
　　Tristrem com that night

[1] test the purity
of.
[2] law.
[3] went.
[4] blame.
[5] marches.
[6] in poor weed
clad.

—Of alle the knightes here
  No knew him non bi sight
    Bidene—
To swete Ysonde bright,
As forward[1] was hem bitvene.

[1] tryst.

Ouer Temes she schuld ride,
  That is an arm of the se:
"To the schip side,
  This man schal bere me."
Tristrem hir bar that tide,
  And on the quen fel he,
Next her naked side
  That mani man might y se
    San schewe[2].

[2] without being
shown.

* .   *   *   *

*   *   *   *   *

In water thai wald him sink,
  And wers[3], yif thai may.
"Ye quite him iuel his swink[4];"
  The quen seyd to hem ay;
"It semeth mete no drink
  Hadde he not mani aday;
For pouerte[5], methenk,
  He fel, for sothe to say,
    And nede[6]:
Yeueth[7] him gold, Y pray,
He may bidde god me spede."

[3] worse.

[4] Ye requite him
ill his toil.

[5] poverty.

[6] want.

[7] Give.

Gold thai youen him thare:
  The constori[1] thai bigan.
Swete Ysonde sware
  Sche was giltles woman;
" Bot on[2] to schip me bare,
  The knightes seighe wele than[3];
What so his wille ware,
  Ferli neighe he wan[4].
      Sothe thing[5],
  So neighe com neuer man
Bot mi lord the king."

Swete Ysonde hath sworn
  Hir clene, that miri may;
To hir thai had y corn[6]
  Hot yren, Y say.
The knightes were bi forn[7];
  For hir tho praiden thai[8].
The yren sche hadde y born,
  Ac Mark foryaue[9] that day
      And dede.
  Meriadok held thai,
For fole in his falshede.

Ysonde is graunted clene,
  Meriadok maugre his[10];
Neuer er nas the quene
  So wele with Mark, Y wis.
Tristrem, with outen wene,
  Into Wales he is;

1 consistory (a bishop's court.)

2 one.

3 saw well then.

4 Strangely nigh he won.

5 A true thing I say.

6 appointed.

7 before, forward.

8 then prayed they.

9 But Mark forgave.

10 In spite of Meriadok his (accusation).

In bataile he hath ben,
And fast he fraines[1] this
Right thare :
For he ne may Ysonde kisse
Fight he sought ay whare.

[1] eagerly he seeks.

Ysonde of the White Hand.

[After famous exploits in Wales, where he relieves the kingdom from the tyranny of a giant, Urgan, Tristrem is invited back to court; but fresh amours with the queen appearing, Mark banishes the two together. They find a dwelling in the forest for a year, till the king, hunting one day, finds them asleep with a drawn sword lying between them. Persuaded of their innocence by this chance circumstance, and enamoured once more by the beauty of Ysonde, he stops with his glove a sunbeam falling through a cranny on her face, and presently recalls his wife and nephew to court. Again surprised by a dwarf, however, in a stolen interview with the queen, Tristrem is compelled to fly.]

Tristrem is went oway
Withouten coming oyain,
And siketh, for sothe to sain[2],
With sorwe and michel[3] pain.
Tristrem fareth ay
As man that wald be slain,
Bothe night and day,
Fightes for to frain[4],
That fre ;
. Spaine he hath thurch sayn[5],
Geauntes he slough thre[6].

[2] sighs, truth to say.
[3] much.

[4] seek.

[5] seen.
[6] Giants three he slew.

Into Bretein he ches[7]
Bi come the doukes knight ;
He set his lond in pes[8],
That arst[9] was ful of fight.

[7] chose.

[8] peace.
[9] formerly.

Al that the doukes wes
   He wan oyain with right.
He bede[1] him, with outen les[2],
   His douhter that was bright
         In land.
That maiden Ysonde hight
With the White Hand.

Tristremes loue was strong
   On swete Ysonde the quene;
Of Ysonde he made a song,
   That song Ysonde bidene.
The maiden wende[3] al wrong
   Of hir it hadde y bene.
Hir wening[4] was so long,
   To hir fader hye gan mene[5]
         For nede.
   Ysonde with hand schene[6]
Tristrem to wiue thai bede[7].

Tristrem a wil is inne,
   Has founden in his thought[8]:
" Mark, mi nem, hath sinne,
   Wrong he hath wrought.
Icham in sorwe and pine,
   Ther to hye hath me brought.
Hir loue, Y say, is mine,
   The boke seyt it is nought[9]
         With right."
   The maiden more he sought
For sche Ysonde hight[10].

[1] offered.
[2] " without lies,
   i.e., in fact.

[3] weened,
   guessed.

[4] desire.

[5] make moan.

[6] fair.

[7] offered.

[8] There is a wish
   in Tristrem
   which he has
   found in his
   thoughts.
   —*M'Neill.*

[9] The Bible saith
   it is not.

[10] was called.

That in his hert he fand,
  And trewely thought he ay;
The torward fast he band[1]
  With Ysonde; that may
With the white hand
  He spoused that day.
O night, Ich vnder stand,
  To boure wenten thai
        On bedde.
Tristrem ring fel oway
As men to chaumber him ledde.

Tristrem bi held that ring,
  Tho was his hert ful wo:
"Oyain me swiche athing
  Dede neuer Ysonde so;
Mark, her lord, the king,
  With tresoun may hir to.
Mine hert may no man bring
  For no thing hir fro,
        That fre.
Ich have tvinned ous to[2],
The wrong is al in me."

Tristrem to bedde yede
  With hert ful of care.
He seyd, "The dern dede[3],
  Do it Y no dare;"
The maiden he for bede[4],
  Yif it hir wille ware.

[1] The compact fast he bound.

[2] I have parted us two.

[3] The secret deed.

[4] demanded.

The maide answerd in lede¹,
" Ther of haue thou no care.
      Al stille
Y nil desiri na mare
      Bot at thine owen wille."

The Suit of Sir Canados.

[Presented with lands by the Duke Florentin of Brittany,
Tristrem is attacked by Beliagog, a neighbouring giant. He
cuts off the giant's foot and compels him to build a splendid hall
containing   in   sculpture   the   whole   history   of   Tristrem.
Presently Ganhardin, brother of Ysonde of the White Hand,
discovers Tristrem's neglect of his sister.   He upbraids the hero,
and   for   answer   is   shown   the   sculptured   hall.   Here   he
acknowledges the superior charms of the Cornish Ysonde, and
becomes so enamoured of the presentment of Brengwain that
Tristrem and he set out for England.   Meanwhile Sir Canados,
a new character, the constable of Mark, seeks to offer his
addresses to the queen.]

Sir Canados was than
      Constable, the quen ful neighe ;
For Tristrem Ysonde wan²,
      So weneth³ he be ful sleighe
To make hir his leman
      With broche and riche beighe⁴.
For nought that he do can,
      Hir hert was euer heighe
            To hold ;
      That man hye never seighe⁵
That bifor Tristrem wold.

² Because
      Tristrem won.
3 thinketh.

4 ring.

5 saw.

Tristrem made asong,
  That song[1] Ysonde the sleighe[2]
And harped euer among.
  Sir Canados was neighe ;
He seyd, " Dame, thou hast wrong,
  For sothe who it seighe.
As oule and stormes strong,
  So criestow on heye
        In herd[3].
  Thou louest Tristrem dreighe[4],
To wrong thou art ylerd[5].

" Tristrem, for thi sake,
  For sothe wiued hath he.
This wil the torn to wrake[6];
  Of Breteyne douke schal he be.
Other semblaunt[7] thou make
  Thiseluen[8], yif thou hir se ;
Thi love hir dede him take,
  For hye hight as do ye[9]
        In land.
  Ysonde men calleth that fre,
With the white hand."

" Sir Canados, the waite[10]!
  Euer thou art mi fo.
Febli thou canst hayte,
  There man schuld menske[11] do.
Who wil lesinges layt[12],
  Tharf him no ferther go.

1 sung.
2 cunning,
    skilful.

3 in public.

4 exceedingly.

5 Thou art
    wrongly in-
    formed.

6 turn to
    vengeance.

7 appearance.

8 Thyself.

9 she is called as
    are ye.

10 guard thee.

11 in manly
    fashion.
12 treachery seek.

1 slander.

2 ever will be to thee sorrow.

3 A curse.

Falsly canestow fayt[1]
  That euer worth the wo[2].
    For thi
  Malisoun[3] haue thou also
Of God and our Leuedy!

"A yift Ich yiue the :

4 Thy good fortune mayst thou lose.

  Thi thrift mot thou tine[4]!
That thou asked me,
  No schal it neuer be thine.
Y hated al so thou be
  Of alle that drink wine!

5 Hence quickly flee.

Hennes yern thou fle[5]
  Out of sight mine
    In lede.
  Y pray to seyn Katerine
That iuel mot thou spede."

The Queen's Tournament.

[Ysonde, disconsolate at the news of Tristrem, betakes herself with Brengwain to the forest. Here they are found by Tristrem returning with his friend. Tristrem and the queen are reconciled, and Brengwain is betrothed to Ganhardin. After spending two days together in the forest the party is nearly surprised by Canados. Coming with the whole force of the country he compels Tristrem and Ganhardin to fly, and carries Ysonde, bitterly upbraiding him, back to court. Tristrem remains in Cornwall, disguised as a beggar, with "cup and clapper." Brengwain, disapproving his conduct, threatens to betray his interviews with Ysonde. Instead, however, she reveals to Mark the presumptuous love of Canados for the queen, and the constable is forthwith banished. Ysonde, fain for her lover, seeks to justify him to Brengwain, and, reduced to flatter her maid, begs her to bring him back. Nevertheless, upon Tristrem's next visit to the queen Brengwain proceeds to taunt him with his late flight.]

Tristrem in bour is blithe,
  With Ysonde playd he thare;
Brengwain badde he lithe[1]:
  "Who ther armes bare,
Ganhardin and thou that sithe[2]
  Wightly oway gun fare[3]."
Quath Tristrem, "Crieth swithe[4]
  A turnament ful yare
        With might:
  Noither of ous nil spare
Erl, baroun, no knight."

[1] bade him listen.

[2] time.

[3] Gallantly fled.

[4] Proclaim quickly.

A turnament thai lete crie;
  The parti Canados tok he[5];
And Meriadok sikerly[6],
  In his help gan he be.
Tristrem ful hastilye,
  Of sent Ganhardin the fre[7];
Ganhardin com titly
  That turnament to se
        With sight;
  Fro the turnament nold thai fle[8]
Til her fon[9] were feld doun right.

[5] Canados took the other side.

[6] surely.

[7] Sent for the noble Ganhardin.

[8] they would not flee.

[9] their foes.

Thai com into the feld,
  And founde ther knightes kene;
Her old dedes thai yeld[10]
  With batayle al bi dene[11].
Tristrem gan bi held,
  To Meriadok bi tvene;

[10] gave up.

[11] speedily.

For the tales he teld,
  On him he wrake his tene[1]
    That tide;
  He yaf him awounde kene
Thurch out bothe side.

[1] wreaked his wrath.

Bitvene Canados and Ganhardin
  The fight was ferly strong;
Tristrem thought it pin[2]
  That it last so long;
His stirops he made him tine[3],
  To grounde he him wrong[4].
Sir Canados ther gan lyn[5],
  The blod thurch brini throng[6].
    With care
  On him he wrake his wrong,
That he no ros na mare.

[2] pain.

[3] lose.

[4] hurled.

[5] lay there.

[6] through helmet pressed.

Her fon fast thai feld[7],
  And mani of hem thai slough;
The cuntre with hem meld[8],
  Thai wrought hem wo ynough.
Tristrem hath hem teld
  That him to schame drough.
Thai token the heighe held[9],
  And passed wele anough,
    And bade.
  Vnder wode bough
After her fomen thai rade.

[7] Their foes eagerly they cast down.

[8] The country with them joined.

[9] took the high keep.

Conclusion.

[Tristrem and Ganhardin, their vengeance accomplished, retire to Brittany. There Tristrem undertakes the aid of a young knight bereft of his mistress. In the combat the young knight is slain. Tristrem avenges his death and slays the fifteen ravishers, but, fatal hap, receives an arrow in his old wound.

At this point the remainder of the romance in the Auchinleck MS. is torn away. Sir Walter Scott in his edition of the poem with curious art supplied a conclusion "in the stile of Thomas of Erceldoune" from two extant fragments of the French metrical version of the tale. This relates how Tristrem's gangrene became daily worse and could be cured by none but Ysonde of Cornwall. Ganhardin, bearing Tristrem's ring, is despatched for the queen, and instructed to hoist a white sail upon his return if accompanied by Ysonde, but a black sail if his embassy be unsuccessful. At last the vessel appears in sight flying a white sail. Ysonde of Brittany, knowing the signal and fired with jealousy, hastens to inform Tristrem. He conjures her to tell him the colour of the sail. She says it is black, whereupon, concluding himself forsaken by Ysonde, Tristrem sinks back in despair and dies. Ysonde of Cornwall lands, and hearing from an old man the death of her lover, rushes to the castle.

> When Ysonde herd that
>   Fast sche gan to gonne,
> At the castel gate
>   Stop hir might none.
> Sche passed in there at,
>   The chaumbre sche won.
> Tristrem in cloth of stat
>   Lay stretched thar as ston
>   So cold.
>   Ysonde loked him on
> And faste gan bihold.
>
> Fairer ladye ere
>   Did Britannye never spye,
> Swiche murning chere
>   Making on heighe.
> On Tristreme's bere
>   Doun con sche lye ;
> Rise ogayn did sche nere,
>   Bot thare con sche dye
>   For woe.
>   Swiche lovers als thei
> Never schal be moe.]

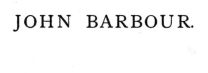

JOHN BARBOUR.

JOHN BARBOUR.

HISTORIAN of the national hero as well as author of
the national epic, John Barbour remains not only the
first but the most famous of the poet-chroniclers of
Scotland. But for his pen the passion of patriotism
which gave Scotland a soul for four hundred years
might have died with Douglas and Bruce, and but
for him the living heroes of the Scottish wars of
succession and independence might have come down
to us little more than empty names.

Considering the fame of his work even in his own
day, it seems strange that hardly anything is known of
the facts of the poet's life. A few dates only have
been discovered here and there, and imagination is
left to clothe these with circumstance. His birth is
set in Aberdeenshire in 1316, two years after the
battle of Bannockburn, but the first certain knowledge
of him does not occur till 1357. His appearance
then is closely connected with the history of the time.
Since the death of Alexander III. force of arms had
been tried by the English kings for the subjugation of
Scotland, and had failed. Now, however, according
to Tytler, " Edward III. seemed to have fallen upon

a more fatal and successful mode of attack." After
eleven years of captivity the Scottish king, David II.,
was held to ransom, and, among other attractions, there
being then no such institutions in their own country,
"the youth of Scotland were induced to frequent the
universities of Oxford and Cambridge by the ready
kindness with which the king gave them letters of
protection." In 1357 Barbour, as Archdeacon of
Aberdeen, was one of the commissioners appointed to
arrange the treaty of ransom at Berwick, and in the
same year and in 1364 he accompanied parties of
young men to Oxford for the purposes of study. His
passports upon these occasions are still extant, "teste
Rege, apud Westmonasterium." There also exist
permits dated 1365 and 1368 allowing him with a
suite to pass through England to France upon
scholarly research. Three times Barbour appears as
one of the auditors of exchequer, and by a charter of
5th December, 1388, he received from Robert II. a
pension of £10 in acknowledgment of his literary ser-
vices. Previously, besides a gift of £10 and a Crown
wardship, he had received a perpetual annuity of 20s.
from his royal master. The annuity he made
over to the chapter of Aberdeen for the saying of an
annual mass for his soul, and regularly till the
Reformation the mass was said in the cathedral there
on the 13th of March. This, accordingly, has been
presumed to be the day of Barbour's death. The
year of his decease has been set at 1395, the last
recorded payment of his larger pension occurring on
3rd April of that year.

Dr. Merry Ross, in his *Scottish History and Litera-ture*, stated somewhat boldly that before the date of Barbour's work the great age of the chroniclers in England was already past. " Besides a solid array of historical names," he adds, " England can show a splendid list of poets, satirists, and critics, when empty silence reigns beyond the Tweed." To some extent, no doubt, this is true, though it was hardly an utter silence which produced *Sir Tristrem* and its following, the ballads of *Ercildoune, Auld Maitland*, and the like, and the other spirited popular poetry which found mention in Gavin Douglas's *Palice of Honour*, and is referred to by Barbour himself.

> Young wemen when thai will play
> Sing it amang them ilk day.

The comparative silence of the north, however, is accounted for by the absence of cohesive nationality. Without this the greatest inspiration of poetry was lacking. No sooner were the various races of Scotland united in a common sympathy by the wars of succession than the national spirit burst full-grown into vigorous poetic flower. In Barbour's *Bruce* appeared, fully developed, the *perfervidum ingenium Scotorum*—no crude fervour, but the earnest, high-hearted enthusiasm for things chivalrous and tender which has been the keynote of Scottish poetry ever since.

The Bruce was not its author's only work. Several passages in Wyntoun's *Cronykil* attest the existence of another :

> This Nynus had a sone alsua,
> Sere Dardane lord de Frygia,

> Fra quham Barbere sutely
> Has made a propyr genealogy
> Tyl Robert oure secownd king
> That Scotland had in governyne.

Again :

> Of Bruttus lyneage quha wyll her,
> He luk the tretis of Barbere
> Mad in-tyl a genealogy
> Rycht wele, and mare perfytly
> Than I can on ony wys
> Wytht all my wyt to yowe dewys.

Barbour himself in *The Bruce*, speaking of the conquests of Arthur, says—

> The Broite beris thairoff wytnes.

This poem, called by Wyntoun elsewhere *The Brut*, has now been completely lost, unless some two thousand lines said to exist in the MS. Troy-books by Lydgate at Cambridge be a part of it. The composition appears to have contained in metre an account of the descent of the Scottish kings from the Trojan Brutus, grandson of Æneas. A work of similar name and purpose was the *Brut* of Layamon in England, and the two are chiefly notable perhaps for showing the praiseworthy desire of all early chroniclers to begin at the beginning of things.

Still another work remains to be attributed to Barbour. Not many years ago Mr. Bradshaw discovered the *Book of Legends of the Saints*. The MS. of this, "a tall, narrow volume, closely written in unmistakably Scottish hand," is now in Cambridge University library, and a printed edition was given to the public in 1889.

But the fame of the Archdeacon of Aberdeen rests with neither of these. It is *The Bruce* which has kept his name shining through the centuries, and it is by *The Bruce* that he will be remembered while the English-speaking race has a heart to be touched and thrilled by generous emotion.

Barbour's poem naturally was neither the first nor the last upon so popular a subject. Patrick Gordon, Gentleman, about 1615 wrote in heroic verse *The Famous History of the Renown'd and Valiant Prince, Robert, Sirnamed the Bruce, King of Scotland,* and in his preface referred to a MS. poem previous to Barbour's. This was by Peter Fenton, a monk in the abbey of Melrose in 1369; but it was tattered and almost illegible when Gordon saw it, and nothing is known of it now.

Of the two manuscripts of Barbour's poem known to exist, one, penned by John Ramsay in 1489, lies now in the Advocates' Library, Edinburgh; the other, dated 1487, and probably by the same hand, as it is signed J. R., is in the archives of St. John's College, Cambridge. By the end of last century there had been made many printed editions " to answer the demand of the common people for this book, which, to the credit of their good sense," said Pinkerton, its editor of 1790, " is very great." Since then there have appeared Dr. Jamieson's edition of 1820, an edition for the Spalding Club by Mr. Cosmo Innes in 1856, and one for the Early English Text Society by the Rev. Mr. Skeat in 1870.

The historical value of *The Bruce* was early recog-

nised. Wyntoun and Boece both excused their
brevity regarding the reign of King Robert by re-
ferring their readers to Barbour.   It is partly
owing, therefore, to the excellence of Barbour's
masterpiece that no other contemporary account
of the period which it records is extant upon the
Scottish side.   On the part of England, it is true,
there exist chronicles like those of Lanercost and of
William of Malmesbury.   These, however, touch only
externally upon matters in which the interests of the
southern kingdom were concerned.   The fact remains
that for the inner atmosphere of Scottish life at the
time, for the detail, character, and circumstance which
give history its meaning, Barbour's *Bruce* is all but the
only source of information.   Nor has the general
truth of his narrative ever been questioned.   Upon
every point but one upon which comparison can be
made his statements accord with otherwise ascertained
facts.   He had every opportunity of acquiring inform-
ation.   The country was ringing from end to end
with details of the great struggle ; at court he was
near the most trustworthy sources of knowledge, and
in his youth at least there must have been about him
many who had ridden by Randolph's side and who
had heard the battle-bugles of the king.   For the
circumstances of Edward Bruce's raid in Galloway he
quotes his actual informant by name :

> A knycht, that then wes in his rowt,
> Worthi and wycht, stalwart and stout,
> Curtaiss, and fayr, and off gud fame,
> Schyr Alane off Catkert by name,
> Tauld me this taile, as I sall tell.

In one conspicuous instance only, as has been said, did Barbour depart from actual fact. With true instinct he perceived the one possible exception which might be taken to his hero's history—the fact that he, bred at Edward's court, had renounced his allegiance; and in order to display briefly the underlying right of Bruce's action he took the liberty of attributing to the grandson the wrong which had been done to the grandfather by the English king. It made a point of poetic justice that the noble who had suffered the wrong should be he who finally took redress at the hands of fortune: whereas it was the grandfather who suffered in Baliol's time and the grandson who triumphed at Bannockburn.

It was not, however, altogether as history that Barbour wrote *The Bruce*. Something of the ancient function of the bard was in his purpose. His intention was the exhibiting of a hero, the stirring of popular enthusiasm, as much as the recording of simple fact. His scheme was larger than mere detail of history. He painted the birth of a nation, and his work remains outstanding among national poems as conspicuously the epic of freedom. The sword had already done its part—Scotland stood erect; it was the poet's time to step forward, to show the true meaning of the struggle which was just over, and to pen its lesson upon the hearts of the people in letters of fire.

None who read *The Bruce* will aver that Barbour failed in what was demanded of him. The awakened soul of the nation was to be kept alive, and, for its

growth in strength and beauty, heroic and gentle ideals
had to be kept before its eyes. These things Barbour
accomplished. It is impossible to estimate the service
to the civilization of his country silently effected by
the praise of such gentle traits as that detailed in the
passage beginning "The king has heard a woman
cry." His work is a gallery of noble portraits, and
when one has closed the book his characters remain
alive in the mind, a strength and an inspiration. On
the southern side Edward I., it is true, is painted all
black, as he appeared to Scottish eyes at that time.
But there is Sir Aymer de Valence, courteous and un-
embittered throughout in face of continued mis-
fortune; and no one can read without a thrill the
farewell of Sir Giles de Argentine to his flying king on
the field of Bannockburn. There is Edward Bruce,
hot-hearted and hot-headed, ever ready to charge
against any odds with no more thought than

> The ma thai be
> The mar honour all out haff we.

There is Douglas, ever full of deft resource, expert in
all arts alike of peace and war, the daring guerilla
chief, gentlest squire of dames, but the terrible "Black
Douglas" in the field. There is Randolph, the king's
nephew, strict in honour as Bruce himself, mettled as
became his princely blood, and wise beyond his age
in governing. There are the gallant young Walter
Stewart and the gentle old bishop, William Lamberton;
the latter heroic through his love for Douglas. Last
and greatest of all appears the hero-king himself,
unmatched in courtesy to noble foes and friends,

terrible beyond telling to traitors, ever ready with the right word or parable to inspire his followers, his every act pregnant with the art of conduct. With rare skill Barbour has shown how the king's greatness made his followers great and inspired the whole hero-ism of his time, so that Sir Ingraham de Umphraville could justly be made to say of him

Ilk yowman is sa wicht
Of his that he is worth a knycht.

The poem should end, perhaps, after the battle of Bannockburn. The object of its action was then attained and its epic meaning complete. There is interior evidence, indeed, that it was originally meant to end here, the date and a general summing up being given. The remainder appears as a sequel, and, like all sequels, possesses diminished interest. The Irish wars of Edward Bruce and the Border exploits of Douglas, well told as they are, lag somewhat after the master-stroke by which the king set firm his throne. For some passages, however, the after part possesses a value of its own, among them being the unique story already referred to of the king's courtesy to women, and a valuable account of the warlike proceedings of that time in a long detailed description of the defence of Berwick.

Of the incidents of the poem, such as Bruce's encouragement of his knights with stories of romance during the tedious crossing of Loch Lomond, Mr. Cosmo Innes has said that "they give us a higher idea of chivalry than any writer of fable has reached." Pinkerton, the earlier editor, took occasion to say that he 'preferred the life, spirit, and ease of Barbour, the plain sense, pictures of real manners, and perpetual incident and entertainment, to the melancholy sublimity of Dante and the amorous quaintness of Petrarch. And of the purely literary part Warton, the historian of English poetry, declared that "Barbour has adorned the English language by a strain of versification, expression, and poetical imagery far superior to his age." When the opportunity occurs, the historian of Bruce has shown that he can touch the details of natural description with a sure hand.

> This wes in the moneth of May,
> Quhen byrdis syngis on ilka spray ;
> Melland thair notis with seymly soune
> For softnes of the suet sesoun ;
> And levys of the branchys spredis,
> And blomys brycht besid thaim bredis ;
> And feldis are strowit with flouris
> Well sawarand, of ser colouris ;
> And all thing worthis blith and gay,
> Quhen that this gude king tuk his way
> To rid southwart.

The poem is rich in shrewd observation of the springs of feeling. There is a quaint philosophy about lines like the following :

> To tell off paynis passyt by
> Plesys to heryng petuisly,
> And to reherss thar auld disese
> Dois thaim oft-syss confort and ese.
> With thi thar-to folow na blame
> Dishonour, wikytnes, na schame.

A certain sort of aphorism, too, is constantly occurring :

> For gud help is in gud begynnyng.
> For gud begynnyng and hardy,

Gyff it be folowit wittily,
May ger oftsyss unlikly thing
Cum to full conabill ending.

Barbour was a scholar, apt with classic allusion, and ready always to justify the action of his characters by a comparison with facts of Greek or Roman history— the resolution of Hannibal, the fate of Alexander or Cæsar, or the habits of Aristotle. Although not altogether free from the superstition of his time— inclined, for instance, to credit the presence of a fiend at the deathbed of Edward I.—he had doubts on such possibilities worthy of a later day.

In one respect at least *The Bruce* may be shown to possess an immense advantage over the great epics of Greece and Rome. The reader has immeasurably greater satisfaction in the success of its hero. In the Scottish poem there is no mean bribing of partizan gods, no unfair interference of a *deus ex machinâ*. All victory is fairly won, and is the natural reward of superior prudence, forethought, and courage. The difference in moral effect which this means may be seen at a glance.

John Barbour, as known by his work, possessed in a superlative degree the poet's heart for appreciating all nobleness; and his epic altogether, with the far-famed panegyric on Freedom which it contains, is hardly to be read yet without catching something of the glow, the high, brave-born enthusiasm of its heroic time.

IN the manuscripts of *The Bruce*, as in other ancient MSS., there is no punctuation. Besides this necessary addition, in the following pages hyphens have been introduced to connect words which now form compounds, such as *in-till* (into), *quhar-euir* (wherever), *euir-mar* (evermore). It is thought unnecessary to burden the margin with translations of familiar peculiarities of Scottish spelling like *quh* for *wh* (quhom for whom), *dd* for *th* (thiddyr for thither), *ch* for *gh* (rycht for right). Words and passages of the text enclosed in brackets are gaps supplied by Dr. Jamieson from the reading of early editions and otherwise. As in the case of *Sir Tristrem*, an effort is made by means of summaries between the selected passages to afford a view of the entire poem.

THE BRUCE.

TORYS to rede ar delitabill,
Supposs[1] that thai be nocht bot fabill :
Than suld storyss that suthfast[2] wer,
And thai war said on gud maner,
Hawe doubill plesance in heryng.
The fyrst plesance is the carpyng[3]
And the tothir the suthfastnes,
That schawys the thing rycht as it wes.
And such thyngis that are likand[4]
Tyll mannys heryng[5] ar plesand.
Tharfor I wald fayne set my will,
Giff my wyt mycht suffice thartill,
To put in wryt a suthfast story,
That it lest ay furth in memory,
Swa that na tyme of lenth it let[6],
Na ger it haly be foryet[7].
For auld storys that men redys
Representis to thaim the dedys
Of stalwart folk that lywyt ar[8],
Rycht as thai than in presence war.
And certes, thai suld weill hawe pryss[9]
That in thair tyme war wycht and wiss[10],

[1] Although.
[2] true.
[3] narration.
[4] agreeable.
[5] To man's hearing.
[6] So that no length of time obstruct it.
[7] Nor cause it wholly be forgot.
[8] lived of yore.
[9] have praise.
[10] strong and wise.

And led thair lyff in gret trawaill,

And oft, in hard stour¹ off bataill,

Wan rycht gret price off chewalry,

And war woydyt off cowardy²;

As wes king Robert off Scotland,

That hardy wes off hart and hand;

And gud Schyr James off Douglas,

That in his tyme sa worthy was,

That off hys price and his bounté³

In fer landis renownyt wes he.

Off thaim I thynk this buk to ma.

Now God gyff grace that I may swa

Tret it and bryng it till endyng

That I say nocht bot suthfast thing!

Scotland under Oppression.

[Upon the death of Alexander III. the barons of Scotland, disagreeing upon the competing claims of Baliol and of Bruce to the throne, invite Edward I. of England to act as arbitrator. To turn the dissension to his own advantage Edward offers the crown to the competitor who will do him sovereign homage. Bruce refuses. Baliol accepts, is made king, but presently on a slight pretext is degraded.]

Quhen Schyr Edward, the mychty king,

Had on this wyss⁴ done his likyng

Off Jhone the Balleoll, that swa sone

Was all defawtyt⁵ and wndone,

To Scotland went he than in hy⁶,

And all the land gan occupy

Sa hale that bath castell and toune

War in-till his possessioune,

[Fra Weik anent[1] Orkenay]
To Mullyr snwk[2] in Gallaway,
And stuffyt[3] all with Ingliss men.
Schyrreffys and bailyheys maid he then,
And alkyn[4] othir officeris
That for to gowern land afferis[5]
He maid off Inglis nation;
That worthyt than sa rych fellone[6],
And sa wykkyt and cowatouss,
And swa hawtane and dispitouss[7],
That Scottis men mycht do na thing
That euir mycht pleyss to thar liking.
Thar wyffis wald thai oft forly[8],
And thar dochtrys[9] dispitusly:
And gyff ony of thaim thair-at war wrath,
Thai watyt[10] hym wele with gret scaith[11];
For thai suld fynd sone enchesone[12]
To put hym to destructione.
And gyff that ony man thaim by
Had ony thing that wes worthy,
As horss or hund or othir thing
That war plesand to thar liking,
With rycht or wrang it have wald thai.
And gyf ony wald thaim withsay[13],
Thai suld swa do, that thai suld tyne[14]
Othir land or lyff, or leyff in pyne.
For thai dempt[15] thaim eftir thair will,
Takand na kep to rycht na skill[16].
A! quhat thai dempt them felonly[17]!
For gud knychtis that war worthy,
For litill enchesoune or than nane

1 From Wick opposite.
2 point.
3 furnished.

4 all kinds of.
5 pertains.

6 Who became then so extremely rich.

7 haughty and despiteful.

8 lie with.
9 daughters.

10 plundered.
11 hurt.
12 reason.

13 gainsay.

14 lose.

15 doomed.

16 Taking no heed of right or reason.
17 cruelly.

Thai hangyt be the nekbane.
Als that folk that euir wes fre
And in fredome wount for to be,
Throw thar gret myschance and foly
War tretyt than sa wykkytly
That thair fays thair jugis war.
Quhat wrechitnes may man have mar?

A! fredome is a noble thing!
Fredome mayss man to haiff liking[1].
Fredome all solace to man giffis.
He levys at ess that frely levys!
A noble hart may haiff nane ess,
Na ellys nocht that may him pless,
Gyff fredome failyhe: for fre liking
Is yharnyt our[2] all othir thing.
Na he that ay hass levyt fre
May nocht knaw weill the propyrté[3],
The angyr[4], na the wrechyt dome,
That is cowplyt to foule thyrldome[5].
Bot gyff he had assayit it,
Than all perquer he suld it wyt[6];
And suld think fredome mar to pryss[7]
Than all the gold in warld that is.
Thus contrar thingis euir-mar
Discoweryngis off the tothir ar[8].
And he that thryll is has nocht his;
All that he hass embandownyt is
Till hys lord, quhat-euir he be.
Yheyt has he nocht sa mekill fre[9]
As fre wyll to leyve or do

[1] pleasure.

[2] Is yearned for above.

[3] peculiar state.

[4] grief.

[5] coupled with foul thraldom.

[6] by heart he should know it.

[7] praise, prize.

[8] Revealers of the other are.

[9] not so much free.

That at hys hart hym drawis to.
Than mayss clerkis questioun,
Quhen thai fall in disputacioun,
That gyff man bad his thryll owcht do,
And in the samyn tym come him to
His wyff, and askyt hym hyr det[1],
Quhethir he his lordis neid suld bet[2],
And pay fryst that he awcht[3], and syne[4]
Do furth his lordis commandyne;
Or leve onpayit his wyff, and do
Thai thingis that commandyt is him to?
I leve all the solucioun
Till thaim that ar off mar renoun.
Bot sen thai mak sic comperyng[5]
Betwix the dettis off wedding[6]
And lordis bidding till his threll;
Ye may weile se, thoucht nane yow tell,
How hard a thing that threldome is.
For men may weile se, that ar wyss,
That wedding is the hardest band
That ony man may tak on hand:
And thryldome is weill wer than deid[7];
For quhill a thryll his lyff may leid
It merrys him, body and banys[8];
And dede anoyis him bot anys[9].
Schortly to say, is nane can tell
The halle[10] conditioun off a threll.

[1] duty.
[2] abate.
[3] owes.
[4] afterwards.
[5] comparison.
[6] duties of marriage.
[7] much worse than death.
[8] mars him, body and bones.
[9] death troubles but once.
[10] whole.

James of Douglas.

[Among sufferers is William of Douglas. He is seized by
Edward and slain in prison, and his lands are given to Lord
Clifford. Fleeing from the country, his son, young James of
Douglas, lives in Paris for nearly three years. Returning then
to see whether he cannot do something to regain his heritage,
he lands at St. Andrews, where he is warmly received by the
bishop. His open heart wins him many friends.]

1 loyal.

2 deigned.

3 falsehood.

4 demeaned in
such fashion.

5 somewhat.

6 lisped.

He wes in all his dedis lele[1];

For him dedeynyeit[2] nocht to dele

With trechery na with falset[3].

His hart on hey honour wes set,

And hym contenyt on sic maner[4]

That all him luffyt that war him ner.

Bot he wes nocht so fayr that we

Suld spek gretly off his beauté.

In wysage wes he sumdeill[5] gray,

And had blak har, as Ic hard say.

Bot off lymmys he wes weill maid,

With banys gret, and schuldrys braiḍ.

His body wes weyll [maid and lenye;]

As thai that saw hym said to me.

Quhen he wes blyth he wes lufly,

And meyk and sweyt in cumpany:

Bot quha in battaill mycht him se

All othir contenance had he.

And in spek wlispyt[6] he sum-deill;

Bot that sat him rycht wondre weill.

Till gud Ector of Troy mycht he

In mony thingis likynt be.

Ector had blak har as he had,

And stark lymmys¹, and rycht weill maid,
And wlyspit alsua as did he,
And wes fulfillyt of leawté²,
And wes curtaiss and wyss and wycht.
Bot off manheid and mekill mycht
Till Ector dar I nane comper,
Off all that euir in warldys wer.
The quethyr in his tyme sa wrocht he
That he suld gretly lovyt be.

He duellyt thar quhill on a tid
The king Eduuard, with mekill prid,
Come to Strevillyne with gret mengye³
For till hald thar ane assemblé.
Thiddirwart went mony baroune;
Byschop Wylyame off Lambyrtoun
Raid thiddyr als, and with him was
This squyer James of Dowglas.
The byschop led him to the king,
And said, " Schyr, heyr I to yow bryng
This child that clemys⁴ your man to be,
And prayis you per cheryté
That ye resave her his homage
And grantis him his herytage."
' Quhat landis clemys he?' said the king.
" Schyr, giff that it be your liking,
He clemys the lordschip off Douglas;
For lord tharoff hys fadyr was."
The king then wrethyt him encrely⁵,
And said, ' Schyr byschop, sekyrly
Gyff thow wald kep thi fewté⁶

¹ strong limbs.

² complete in loyalty.

³ following.

⁴ claims.

⁵ was wroth inwardly (*en cœur*).

⁶ fealty.

Thow maid nane sic speking to me.

1 fierce foe.

Hys fadyr ay wes my fay feloune[1],
And deyt tharfor in my presoun,
And wes agayne my maiesté;
Tharfor hys ayr I aucht to be.
Ga purches land quhar-euir he may;

2 thereof has he none i' faith (*par foi*).

For tharoff haffys he nane perfay[2].
The Clyffurd sall thaim haiff, for he
Ay lely has serwyt to me.'
The byschop hard him swa ansuer,

3 dared.

And durst[3] than spek till him na mar;
Bot fra his presence went in hy,

4 dreaded sore his cruelty.

For he dred sayr his felouny[4]:
Swa that he na mar spak thairto.
The king did that he com to do,
And went till Ingland syn agayn,

5 much strength.

With mony man off mekill mayn[5].

Bruce Defeated.

[Riding from Stirling one day Sir John Cumyn proposes to assist Bruce in a rising. Bruce consents, but the compact is betrayed by Cumyn. Bruce is summoned to London, and, unwitting of treachery, narrowly escapes arrest. He posts north to Lochmaben, raises his vassals, stabs Cumyn at the high altar at Dumfries, and takes the field. He is joined by the young Douglas and crowned at Scone, but is surprised and, in spite of prodigies of personal valour, defeated first at Methven, and afterwards, while wandering with the queen and her ladies among the hills, by John of Lorn at Dalry.]

The king that nycht his wachis set,
And gert ordayne that thai mycht et;
And bad conford to thaim tak,
And at thar mychtis mery mak.

" For disconford," as then said he,
" Is the werst thing that may be.
For throw mekill disconforting
Men fallis off in-to disparyng,
And fra a man disparyt be,
Then trewly wtterly wencusyt[1] is he,   1 vanquished.
And fra the hart be discumfyt,
The body is nocht worth a myt[2].   2 mite.
Tharfor," he said, " atour[3] all thing,   3 above.
Kepys yow fra disparyng,
And thynk thouch we now harmys fele,
That God may yeit releve ws weill.
Men redys off mony men that war
Fer hardar stad[4] then we yhet ar,   4 harder beset.
And syne our lord sic grace thaim lent
That thai come weill till thair entent.

For Rome quhilum sa hard wes stad
Quhen Hanniball thaim wencusyt had,

. . . .

Ye may weill be ensampill se
That na man suld disparyt be,
Na lat his hart be wencusyt all
For na myscheiff that euir may fall.
For nane wate[5] in how litill space   5 know.
That God wmquhile[6] will send grace.   6 sometimes.
Had thai* fled and thar wayis gane
Thar fayis swith[7] the toune had tane.   7 quickly.
Tharfor men that werrayand war[8]   8 carry on war.

*The people of Rome.

1 aim.

Suld set thair etlyng[1] euir-mar
To stand agayne thair fayis mycht,
Wmquhile with strenth and quhile with slycht,
And ay thynk to cum to purpos;

2 choice.

And giff that thaim war set in choss[2]
To dey or to leyff cowartly,

3 rather.

Thai suld erar[3] dey chewalrusly."

4 In this fashion.

Thusgat[4] thaim confort the king,
And to confort thaim gan inbryng
Auld storys off men that wer

5 in several hard
   trials.

Set in-tyll hard assayis ser[5],

6 thwarted.

And that fortoun contraryit[6] fast,
And come to purposs at the last.

The Parting with the Queen.

He prechyt thaim on this maner,

7 feigned.

And fenyeit[7] to mak better cher
Then he had matir to, be fer:

8 went from ill to
   worse.

For his causs yeid fra ill to wer[8].
Thai war ay in sa hard trawaill,
Till the ladyis began to fayle,

9 suffer.

That mycht the trawaill drey[9] na mar.
Sa did othir als that thar war.
The erle Jhone wes ane off tha,
Off Athole, that quhen he saw sua
The king be discumfyt twyss,

And sa feile[1] folk agayne him ryss,

And lyff in sic trawaill and dout,

IIis hart begane to faile all out.

And to the king apon a day

He said, "Gyff I durst to yow say,

We lyff in to sa mekill dreid,

And haffis oft-syss[2] off met sic ned,

And is ay in sic trawailling,

With cauld and hungir and waking,

That I am sad off my-selwyn[3] sua

That I count nocht my liff a stra.

Thir angrys[4] may I ne mar drey,

For thoucht me tharfor worthit dey.

I mon soiourne, quhar-euir it be.

Leuys me[5] tharfor per cheryté."

The king saw that he sa wes failyt,

And that he ik wes for trawaillyt[6].

He said, "Schyr erle, we sall sone se

And ordayne how it best may be.

Quhar-euyr ye be, our Lord yow send

Grace fra your fais yow co defend!"

With that in hy to him callyt he

Thaim that till him war mast priué:

Then amang thaim thai thocht it best,

And ordanyt for the liklyest,

That the queyne and the erle alsua

And the ladyis in hy[7] suld ga

With Nele the Bruce till Kildromy.

For thaim thocht thai mycht sekyrly[8]

Duell thar quhill thai war wictaillit weile.

For swa stalwart wes the castell

[1] many.

[2] often.

[3] myself.

[4] These griefs.

[5] Give me leave.

[6] also was sore fatigued.

[7] in haste.

[8] securely.

That it with strenth war hard to get
Quhill that thar-in wer men and mete.
As thai ordanyt thai did in hy:
The queyne and all hyr cumpany
Lap[1] on thair horss and furth thai far.
Men mycht haiff sene, quha had bene thar,
At leve-takyng the ladyis gret[2]
And mak thar face with teris wet,
And knychtis for thar luffis sak
Bath sich and wep and murnyng mak.
Thai kyssyt thair luffis at thair partyng.
The king wmbethocht him off a thing;
That he fra thine on fute wald ga,
And tak on fute bath weill and wa,
And wald na horss-men with him haiff.
Tharfor his horss all haile[3] he gaiff
To the ladyis that mystir[4] had.
The queyn furth on hyr wayis rade,
And sawffly come to the castell,
Quhar hyr folk war ressawyt weill
And esyt weill with meyt and drynk.
Bot mycht nane eyss let[5] hyr to think
On the king that wes sa sar stad
That bot twa hundre with him had.
The quhethir thaim weill confortyt he ay:
God help him, that all mychtis may!

1 Leaped.

2 weep.

3 all whole, every one.
4 necessity.

5 no ease might prevent.

The King a Fugitive.

[Bruce with his two hundred men wanders for a time among the mountains, but, winter coming on, he determines to retreat to Kintyre. He sends Sir Neil Campbell in advance to procure provision.]

The king, eftir that he wes gane,
To Lowchlomond the way has tane[1]   [1] taken.
And come thar on the thrid day.
Bot thar-about na bait fand thai[2]   [2] no boat found
That mycht thaim our the water ber.   they.
Than war thai wa[3] on gret maner,   [3] woful.
For it wes fer about to ga,
And thai war in to dout alsua
To meyt thair fayis that spred war wyd.
Tharfor endlang[4] the louchhis syd   [4] along.
Sa besyly thai socht and fast,
Tyll Jamys of Dowglas at the last
Fand a litill sonkyn bate
And to the land it drew fut hate[5].   [5] straightway
Bot it sa litill wes that it   (hot-foot).
Mycht our the watter bot thresum flyt[6].   [6] transport but
Thai send tharoff word to the king,   three together.
That wes joyfull off that fynding;
And fyrst in-to the bate is gane,
With him Dowglas. The thrid wes ane
That rowyt thaim our deliuerly[7]   [7] nimbly.
And set thaim on the land all dry,
And rowyt sa oft-syss to and fra,
Fechand ay our twa and twa,
That in a nycht and in a day

Cummyn owt-our the louch ar thai.
For sum off thaim couth swome full weill
And on his bak ber a fardele[1].
Swa with swymmyng and' with rowyng
Thai brocht thaim our, and all thair thing.

[1] a burden.

The king, the quhilis, meryly
Red to thaim that war him by
Romanys off worthi Ferambrace,*
That worthily our-cummyn[2] was
Throw the rycht douchty Olywer;
And how the Duk Peris[3] wer
Assegyt[4] in-till Egrymor.

[2] overcome.

[3] the Twelve Peers of France (Douze Pairs).
[4] besieged.

The Death of Edward I.

[Bruce betakes himself to winter at the Isle of Rachryn. The queen and her daughter, leaving shelter, are made prisoners at the Girth of Tain, and Kildromy itself, after a gallant defence by Neil Bruce, is betrayed and reduced by the English.]

Bot quhen the king Eduuard hard say
How Neill the Bruce held Kildromy
Agayne his sone sa stalwartly,
He gaderyt gret chewalry
And towart Scotland went in hy.

And as in-till Northummyrland
He wes with his gret rowt ridand,
A seknes tuk him in the way,

*_Sir Fierabras_, one of the romances concerning Charlemagne and his twelve peers. It was edited from the Ashmole MS. by Mr. Sidney J. Herrtage for the Early English Text Society in 1879.

And put him to sa hard assay
That he mycht nocht ga na ryd.
Him worthit, magre his[1], abid   1 It behoved him,
In-till an hamillet thar-by,   despite his
A litill toun and wnworthy.   (desire).
With gret payne thiddir thai him broucht;
He wes sa stad that he ne mocht
Hys aynd bot[2] with gret paynys draw,   2 His own boot.
Na spek bot giff it war weill[3] law.   3 actually.
The quhethir he bad thai suld him say
Quhat toun wes that, that he in lay.
" Schyr," thai said, " Burch in the Sand
Men callis this toun, in-till this land."
' Call thai it Burch? Alas!' said he,
' My hop is now fordone[4] to me.   4 quite worn out.
For I wend neuir to thoile[5] the payne   5 weened never
Off deid till I, throw mekill mayn,   to suffer.
The Burch off Jerusalem had tane.
My lyff wend I thar suld be gayne[6].   6 finished.
In Burch I wyst weill I suld de,
Bot I was nothir wyss na sle[7]   7 cunning.
Till othyr Burch kep to ta[8].   8 to take excep-
' Now may I na-wiss forthyr ga.'   tion.
Thus pleynyeit[9] he off his foly,   9 complained.
As he had mater sckyrly[10]   10 surely.
Quhen he cowyt[11] certanté   11 coveted.
Off that at nane may certan be.

[Edward, it appears, had consulted a certain fiend as to the
date and place of his death, and the familiar, after the manner of
his kind, had deceived his patron with an equivocal answer.]

At Jerusalem trowyt[12] he   12 trusted.
Grawyn[13] in the Burch to be ;   13 Interred.

The quethyr at Burch in-to the Sand

¹ died.

He swelt¹ rycht in his awn land.
And quhen he to the dede wes ner,
The folk, that at Kyldromy wer,
Come with prisoneris that thai had tane,
And syne to the king ar gane.
And for to confort him thai tauld

² yielded.

How thai the castell to thaim yauld²;
And how thai till his will war broucht,
To do off that quhat-euir he thoucht;
And askyt quhat men suld off thaim do.
Then lukyt he angyrly thaim to,

³ Hang and draw.

And said grynnand, " Hyngis and drawys³."

⁴ such a saying.

That wes wondir of sic sawis⁴,
That he, that to the dede was ner,
Suld answer apon sic maner,

⁵ Without compassion.

For-owtyn menyng⁵ and mercy;
How mycht he traist on hym to cry,

⁶ truly judges.

That suthfastly demys⁶ all thing,
To haiff mercy for his criyng,
Off him that, throw his felony,

⁷ In such state of body.

In-to sic poynt⁷ had na mercy?
His men his maundment has done,
And he deyt thareftir sone,

⁸ burial.

And syne wes broucht till berynes⁸.
His sone syne king eftir wes.

The Return of the King.

[Douglas, irking at idleness and pitying the burdened islanders, leaves Rachryn, makes a descent upon Arran, succeeds in cutting off a convoy of supplies, and all but takes the castle of Brodick. Ten days later Bruce sets sail.]

With thretty small galayis and thre
The king arywyt[1] in Arane,   1 arrived.
And syne[2] to the land is gane   2 presently.
And in a toune tuk his herbery[3],   3 took quarters in in a hamlet.
And speryt[4] syne speceally   4 inquired.
Gyff ony man couth tell tithand[5]   5 tidings.
Off ony strang men in that land.
"Yhis," said a woman, "Schyr, perfay,
Off strang men I kan yow say,
That ar cummyn in this countré,
And schort quhile syne, throw thair bounté,
Thai haff discomfyt our wardane,
And mony off his men has slane.
And till a stalwart place herby
Reparis all thair cumpany."
'Dame,' said the king, 'wald thow we wiss[6]   6 direct us.
To that place quhar thair repair[7] is,   7 gathering.
I sall reward the but lesing[8];   8 without fraud, indeed.
For thai ar all off my duelling,
And I rycht blythly wald them se,
And swa trow I that thai wald me.'
"Yhis," said scho, "Schyr, I will blythly
Ga with yow and your cumpany,
Till that I schaw yow thair repair."
'That is inewch[9], my systir fayr;   9 enough.

'Now ga we forthwart,' said the king.
Than went thai furth but mar letting[1],
Folowand her as scho thaim led,
Till at the last scho schawyt a sted[2]
To the king in a wode glen,
And said, "Schyr, her I saw the men
That yhe sper eftir mak logyng;
Her I trow be thair reparying."

The king then blew his horn in hy,
And gert[3] the men that wer him by
Hald thaim still and all priwé;
And syne agayn his horn blew he.
James of Dowglas herd him blaw,
And at the last alsone[4] gan knaw,
And said, "Sothly yon is the king:
I knaw lang quhill syne[5] his blawyng."
The thrid tym thar with all he blew,
And then Schyr Robert Boid it knew,
And said, "Yone is the king but dreid[6];
Ga we furth till him bettir speid."
Than went thai till the king in hy,
And him inclynyt curtasly.
And blythly welcummyt thaim the king,
And wes joyfull of thair meting,
And kissit thaim, and speryt syne
How thai had farne[7] in thair huntyn.
And thai him tauld all but lesing:
Syne lowyt[8] thai God off thair meting.
Syne with the king till his herbery
Went bath joyfull and joly.

[1] without more delay.
[2] showed a place.
[3] caused.
[4] as soon as the last (blast sounded).
[5] long time since.
[6] without doubt.
[7] fared.
[8] praised.

The Landing in Carrick.

[A council of war is held, and a descent upon the opposite mainland determined. Cuthbert, a scout, is sent over to Carrick with orders if landing appears feasible to light a fire on Turnberry Head. On the appointed day the fire is seen. As the king prepares to leave the beach a woman beckons him apart and in a spirited harangue prophesies his approaching triumph. He then sets sail.]

This wes in ver[1], quhen wyntir-tid,	1 spring.
With his blastis hidwyss to bid[2],	2 hideous to abide.
Was our-drywyn[3], and byrdis smale,	3 over-driven.
As turturis and the nychtyngale,	
Begouth rycht sariely[4] to syng,	4 Began right artfully.
And for to mak in thair singyng	
Swete notis, and sownys ser[5],	5 sounds many.
And melodys plesand to her;	
And the treis begouth to ma	
Burgeans[6], and brycht blomys alsua,	6 Buds.
To wyn the helyng off thair hewid[7]	7 To get the covering of their head.
That wykkyt wyntir had thaim rewid[8];	8 reft.
And all gressys beguth to spryng.	
In-to that tyme the nobill king,	
With his flote and a few mengye,	
Thre hundyr I trow thai mycht be,	
Is to the se, owte off Arane,	
A litill forouth ewyn gane[9].	9 gone forth in even array.
Thai rowit fast with all thair mycht	
Till that apon thaim fell the nycht,	
That woux myrk[10] apon gret maner,	10 waxed dark.
Swa that thai wyst nocht quhar thai wer.	

For thai na nedill had, na stane,

[1 in one body.] Bot rowt alwayis in-till ane[1],

Sterand all tyme apon the fyr

[2 clear.] That thai saw brynnand lycht and schyr[2].

[3 adventure.] It wes bot auentur[3] thaim led,

And thai in schort tyme sa thaim sped

That at the fyr arywyt thai,

And went to land but mar delay.

And Cuthbert, that has sene the fyr,

[4 grief.] Was full off angyr[4] and off ire:

For he durst nocht do it away,

And wes alsua dowtand ay

That his lord suld pass to se.

Tharfor thair cummyn waytit he,

And met thaim at thair arywing.

He wes wele sone broucht to the king,

That speryt at hym how he had done.

And he with sar hart tauld him sone

[5 well-disposed.] How that he fand nane weill luffand[5],

Bot all war fayis that he fand:

And that the lord the Persy,

With ner thre hundre in cumpany,

Was in the castell thar besid,

[6 "choke-full."] Fullfillyt[6] off dispyt and prid;

Bot ma than twa partis off his rowt

[7 quartered in the steading.] War herberyt in the toune[7] without:

" And dyspytyt yow mar, Schir king,

Than men may dispyt ony thing."

Than said the king, in full gret ire,

'Tratour, quhy maid thow than the fyr?'

" A! Schyr," said he, " sa God me se!

The fyr wes newyr maid for me.
Na, or[1] the nycht, I wyst it nocht;
Bot fra[2] I wyst it, weill I thocht
That ye and haly your menye
In hy suld put yow to the se.
For-thi[3] I cum to mete yow her,
To tell perellys that may aper."

1 ere.
2 from the time when.
3 therefore.

The king wes off his spek angry,
And askyt his prywé men, in hy,
Quhat at thaim thoucht wes best to do.
Schyr Edward fryst answert thar-to,
Hys brodyr that wes swa hardy,
And said, "I say yow sekyrly
Thar sall na perell that may be
Dryve me eftsonys[4] to the se.
Myne auentur her tak will I,
Quhethir it be esfull or angry."
'Brothyr,' he said, 'sen thou will sua,
It is gud that we saymn ta[5]
Dissese or ese, or payne or play,
Eftyr as God will ws purway.
And sen men sayis that the Persy
Myn heretage will occupy,*
And his menye sa ner ws lyis,
That ws dispytis mony wyss,
Ga we and wenge sum off the dispyte;
And that may we haiff done alss tite[6],
For thai ly traistly, but dreding[7]

4 presently.

5 together take.

6 also soon.
7 trustfully, without fear.

* Bruce inherited Carrick through his mother, whose first husband had been earl of that district.

Off ws or off our her cummyng.
And thoucht we slepand slew thaim all,
Repruff tharoff na man sall.
For werrayour na forss[1] suld ma,
Quhethir he mycht ourcum his fa
Throw strenth or throw sutelté,
Bot that gud faith ay haldyn be.'

[1] warrior no scruple.

The Defence at the Ford.

[Percy abandons Turnberry. A lady of the country, cousin to Bruce, joins the king with forty followers and informs him of the fall of Kildromy and the taking of the queen. Douglas, obtaining permission, departs alone for Douglasdale, declares himself to his people, and surprising his enemies at kirk on Palm Sunday, puts them to the sword. His slaughter of prisoners among the meal and wine on the castle floor is called "The Douglas Larder." Meanwhile the king, attacked by traitors in a covert, excites his followers' admiration by his single-handed defence.

Presently the men of Galloway, seeing him with but few retainers, come upon him suddenly, two hundred strong.]

Thai schup thaim in an ewynnyng[2]
To suppriss[3] sodanly the king;
And till him held thai straucht thair way.
Bot he, that had his wachis ay
On ilk[4] sid, off thair cummyng,
Lang or thai come, had wytterịng[5],
And how fele[6] that thai mycht be.
Tharfor he thoucht, with his menye,
To withdraw him out off the place,
For the nycht weill fallyn was.
And for the nycht he thoucht at[7] thai

[2] prepared on an evening.
[3] suppress.
[4] every.
[5] information.
[6] many.
[7] that.

Suld nocht haiff sycht to hald the way
That he war passyt with his menye.
And as he thoucht rycht swa did he,
And went him doun till a morrass,
Our a wattyr that rynnand was;
And in the bog he fand a place
Weill strait, that weill twa bow-drawcht[1] was   [1] quite two bow-shots.
Fra the wattyr thai passit haid.
He said, " Her may ye mak abaid,
And rest yow all a quhile and ly.
I will ga wach all priuely
Giff Ik her oucht off thair cummyng :
And giff I may her ony thing,
I sall ger warn you, sa that we
Sall ay at our awantage be."

The king now takys his gate[2] to ga,   [2] takes his way.
And with him tuk he sergeandis twa[3];   [3] two squires.
And Schyr Gilbert de la Hay left he
Thar, for to rest with his menye.
To the wattyr he come in hy,
And lysnyt full ententily
Giff he herd oucht off thair cummyng ;
Bot yeit mocht he her na thing.
Endlang the wattyr than yeid he[4]   [4] Along the stream then went he.
On athyr syd a gret quantité,
And saw the brayis[5] hey standand,   [5] hillsides.
The wattyr holl throw slik rynnand[6];   [6] The deep water running through slime.
And fand na furd that men mycht pass,
Bot quhar him-selwyn[7] passit was.   [7] himself.
And swa strait wes the wpcummyng

That twa men mycht nocht samyn thring[1],
Na on na maner press thaim swa
That thai to-gidder mycht lang ga.

And quhen he a lang quhile had bene thar
He herknyt, and herd as it war
A hundis questionyng on fer[2],
That ay come till him ner and ner.
He stude still, for till herkyn mar,
And ay the langer he wes thar
He herd it ner and ner cummand.
Bot he thocht he thar still wald stand,
Tyll that he heard mar takynnyng[3],
Than, for ane hundis questionyng,
He wald nocht wakyn his menye.
Tharfor he wald abid, and se
Quhat folk thai war, and quhethir thai
Held towart him the rycht way,
Or passyt ane othyr way fer by.
The moyne wes schynand clerly.
Sa lang he stude, that he mycht her
The noyis off thaim that cummand wer
Than his twa men in hy[4] send he
To warne and walkyn his menye[5];
And thai ar furth thair wayis gane
And he left thar all hym allane.
And swa stude he herknand,
Till that he saw cum at his hand
The hale rout, in-till full gret hy.
Then he wmbethoucht him hastily
Giff he held towart his menye

Marginal notes:

1 thrust together.

2 A hound's bay-
ing far off.

3 betokening.

4 in haste.

5 waken his fol-
lowing.

That, or he mycht reparyt be[1],
Thai suld be passit the furd ilkan[2].
And then behutfyt him chess ane
Off thir twa, othyr to fley or dey.
Bot his hart that wes stout and hey
Consaillyt hym hym allane to bid,
And kepe thaim at the furde syd,
And defend weill the wpcummyng;
Sen he was warnyst of armyng[3]
That he thar arowys thurch nocht dreid.
And gyff he war off gret manheid
He mycht stunay thaim euirilkane[4],
Sen thai ne mycht cum bot ane and ane.
He did rycht as hys hart hym bad.
Strang wtrageouss curage he had,
Quhen he sa stoutly him allane,
For litill strenth off erd[5], has tane
To fecht with twa hundre and ma.
Thar-with he to the furd gan ga,
And thai, apon the tothyr party,
That saw him stand thar anyrly[6],
Thringand[7] in-till the wattyr rad.
For off him litill dout thai had,
And raid till him in full gret hy.
He smate the fyrst swa wygorusly
With his sper, that rycht scharp schar[8],
Till he doun till the erd him bar.
The lave[9] come then in-till a randoun[10];
Bot his horss, that wes born doun,
Combryt thaim the wpgang to ta[11].
And quhen the king saw it was swa,

[1] ere he might join his men.
[2] each one.
[3] furnished with armour.
[4] dismay them every one.
[5] ground.
[6] alone.
[7] Thronging.
[8] cut.
[9] remainder.
[10] torrent.
[11] Cumbered them in the ascent.

He stekyt[1] the horss, and he gan flyng,
And syne fell at the wpcummyng.
The layff with that come with a schout;
And he, that stalwart wes and stout,
Met thaim rycht stoutly at the bra,
And sa gud payment gan thaim ma,
That fyvesum in the furd he slew.
The lave then sumdele thaim withdrew,
That dred his strakys wondre sar,
For he in nathing thaim forbar.

Then said ane, " Certes, we ar to blame.
Quhat sall we say quhen we cum hame,
Quhen a man fechtis[2] agane ws all?
Quha wyst euir[3] men sa foully fall
As ws, gyff that we thusgat leve?"
With that all haile[4] a schout thai geve,
And cryit, "On him! he may nocht last."
With that thai pressyt hym sa fast
That had he nocht the better bene
He had bene dede with-owtyn wen[5].
Bot he sa gret defence gan mak
That quhar he hyt ewyn a strak
Thar mycht na thing agane [him] stand.
In litill space he left liand
Sa fele[6] that the wpcummyng wes then
Dyttyt[7] with slayn horss and men;
Swa that his fayis, for that stopping,
Mycht nocht cum to the wpcummyng.

[1] stabbed.
[2] fights.
[3] Whoever knew.
[4] all whole.
[5] without doubt.
[6] So many.
[7] closed up.

A! der God! quha had then bene by,
And sene how he sa hardyly
Addressyt hym agane thaim all,
I wate weile that thai suld him call
The best that levyt in his day.
And giff I the suth sall say,
I herd neuir in na tym gane
Ane stynt[1] sa mony him allane.   [1] stop.

On this manner, that Ik haiff tauld,
The king, that stout wes and bauld,
Wes fechtand on the furd syd,
Giffand and takand rowtis roid[2],   [2] rude blows.
Till he sic. martyrdom thar has maid
That he the ford all stoppyt haid,
That nane off thaim mycht till him rid.
Thaim thoucht than foly for to byd,
And halely the flycht gan ta,
And went hamwartis[3] quhar thai come fra.   [3] homewards.
For the kingis men with the cry
Walknyt full effrayitly[4],   [4] Wakened
                                                       affrightedly.
And com to sek thair lord the king.
The Gallowaymen hard thar cummyng,
And fled, and durst abid no mar.
The kingis men, that dredand war
For thair lord, full spedyly
Come to the furd; and sone in hy
Thai fand the king syttand allane,
That off hys bassynet[5] has tane   [5] helmet.

Till awent[1] him, for he wes hate.
Than speryt thai at him off his state,
And he tauld thaim all hale the cass,
Howgate that he assailyt was,
And how that God him helpyt swa
That he eschapyt hale thaim fra.
Than lukyt thai how fele war ded;
And thai fand lyand in that sted
Fourtene, that war slayne with his hand.

Than lovyt[2] thai God fast[3], all weildand[4],
That thai thair lord fand hale and fer;
And said thaim byrd[5] on na maner
Drede thair fayis, sen thair chyftane
Wes off sic hart and off sic mayn
That he for thaim had wndretan

With swa fele for to fecht ane[6].

Syk wordis spak thai of the king,
And for his hey wndretaking
Farlyit[7], and yarnyt hym for to se,
That with him ay wes wont to be.

A! quhat worschip is perfyt thing[8]!
For it mayss men till haiff loving[9],
Giff it be folowit ythenly[10].
For pryce off worschip nocht-forthi[11]
Is hard to wyn. For gret trawaill,
Offt to defend and oft assaill,
And to be in thair dedis wyss,
Gerris men off worschip wyn the pryce.

The Goodwife of Carrick.

[The English warden, Sir Aymer de Valence, determined on a decisive blow, approaches with a great force. The king attacks him, but finds himself in turn attacked behind by John of Lorn with eight hundred men. Seeing the odds hopeless, he divides his following into three parties to distract pursuit. Again and again this device is resorted to, but John of Lorn, with a bloodhound, continually pursues the king's company. At last Bruce, left alone with his foster-brother, slays with his own hand four of five pursuers who overtake him. Then, losing heart, he declares he will go no further. But the foster-brother rallies him, and presently he remembers a device. Wading a bowshot down a running stream they throw the hound off the scent and escape. In this fight, it is said, Thomas Randolph on the English side won great honour by capturing Bruce's banner. The king and his man the same night are attacked when asleep by three assassins. The foster-brother is slain, but Bruce avenges his death on the three traitors. Afterwards he sets forth towards his tryst.]

The king went furth way and angry[1],	[1] woful and grieved.
Menand[2] his man full tendirly;	[2] lamenting.
And held his way, all him allane,	
And rycht towart the houss is gan	
Quhar he set tryst to meit his men.	
It wes weill inwith[3] nycht be then.	[3] towards.
He come sone in the houss, and fand	
The howsswyff on the benk[4] sittand;	[4] bench.
That askit him quhat he was,	
And quhen[5] he come, and quhar he gas.	[5] whence.
"A trawailland man, dame," said he,	
"That trawaillys her throw the contré."	
Scho said, 'All that trawailland er,	
For ane his sak, ar welcum her.'	
The king said, "Gud dame, quhat is he	
That gerris yow haiff sic specialté[6]	[6] peculiar regard.
To men that trawaillis?" 'Schyr, perfay,'	

Quoth the gud wyff, 'I sall yow say.
The king, Robert the Bruyss, is he,
That is rycht lord off this countré.

1 struggle. His fayis now haldis him in thrang[1];

2 ere any length of time. Bot I think to se or ocht lang[2]
Him lord and king our all the land,
That na fayis sall him withstand.'
"Dame, luffis thow him sa weil?" said he.
'Ya Schyr,' said scho, 'so God me se!'
"Dame," sayd he, "[lo] hym her the by;

3 truly. For Ik am he, I say the soithly[3];
Yha certes, dame." 'And quhar are gane
Your men, quhen ye ar thus allane?'

4 more. "At this time, dame, Ik haiff no ma[4]."
Scho said; 'It may na-wyss be swa.
Ik haiff twa sonnys, wycht and hardy;
Thai sall becum your men in hy.'

5 devised. As scho diuisyt[5] thai haiff done;
His sworne men become thai sone.
The wyff syn gert him syt and ete;
Bot he has schort quhile at the mete
Syttyn, quhen he hard gret stamping
About the howss. Then, but letting,
Thai stert wp the howss for to defende.
That sone eftre the king has kend
James off Dowglas. Than wes he blyth,

6 quickly. And bad oppyn the durris swyth[6].
And thai cum in, all that thar war.
Schyr Eduuard the Bruce wes thar,
And James alsua of Dowglas,
That wes eschapyt fra the chace

And with the kingis brothyr met.

Syn to the tryst that thaim wes set

Thai sped thaim with thair cumpany,

That war ane hundir and weile fyfty.

Edward Bruce in Galloway.

[Successful in several minor engagements and in repulsing
another private attack upon his life, the king determines to essay
greater things.   A detachment of a thousand men under Sir
Philip Mowbray, coming from Bothwell to surprise him, are
waylaid by Douglas near Kilmarnock and put to rout.   Bruce
then accepts a challenge from De Valence to join battle under
Loudon Hill.   Beforehand he takes care to manipulate the field
so that the forces will meet on something like equal footing, and
the result is the final overthrow of the English warden.   Setting
out forthwith to meet the hostile lords in the north, the king
falls seriously ill.   He is carried from place to place in a litter,
and his friends begin to lose heart, till one day, his forces being
attacked at Old Meldrum by Sir David of Brechin, he calls for
his horse and armour, and routs at once his sickness and his
enemies.   Forfar Castle is taken and demolished, and Perth,
after a six weeks' siege, falls before the king's attack in person.
Meanwhile in the south Douglas has again by stratagem taken
and destroyed his own castle, and Edward Bruce has set forth to
free Galloway.   After routing a large force by the Water of
Cree he does not hesitate with only fifty men to fall upon
fifteen hundred.]

Throw his chewalrouss chewalry

Galloway wes stonayit gretumly[1],

And he dowtyt for his bounté[2].

Sum off the men off the countré

Come till his pess, and maid him aith.

Bot Schyr Amery, that had the skaith[3]

Off the bargane[4] I tauld off er,

Raid till Ingland till purches ther

Off armyt men gret cumpany,

To weng him off the welany[5]

[1] greatly dis-
mayed.
[2] feared for his
worth.

[3] hurt.
[4] fight.

[5] avenge the
disgrace.

That Schyr Eduuard, that noble knycht,
Him did by Cre in-to the fycht.
Off gud men he assemblit thar
Weill fyftene hundyr men and mar
That war off rycht gud renowmé.
His way with all that folk tuk he,
And in the land all priuely
Entryt with that chewalry,
Thynkand Schyr Eduuard to suppryss,
Giff that he mowcht on ony wiss.
For he thoucht he wald him assaile,
Or that he left, in playn bataill.

¹ wonder.

Now may ye her off gret ferly¹
And off rycht hey chewalry.
For Schyr Eduuard in-to the land
Wes, with his mengné, rycht ner hand,
And in the mornyng rycht arly
Herd the countré men mak cry,
And had wyttryng off thair cummyng.
Than buskyt he him, but delaying,

² nimbly.

And lapp on horss delyuerly².
He had than in route fyfty,
All apon gud horss armyt weill.

³ caused he each one.

His small folk gert he ilkdeill³
Withdraw thaim till a strait tharby,
And he raid furth with his fyfty.

A knycht that then wes in his rowt,

⁴ Valorous.
⁵ proper.

Worthi⁴ and wycht, stalwart and stout,
Curtaiss and fayr⁵ and off gud fame,

Schyr Alane off Catkert by name,
Tauld me this taile, as I sall tell.
Gret myst in-to the morning fell,
Sa thai mycht nocht se thaim by,
For myst, a bowdraucht fullely.
Sa hapnyt it that thai fand the traiss,
Quhar-at the rowte furth passyt waiss
Off thair fayis, that forowth raid[1].   [1] rode before.
Schyr Eduuard, that gret yarnyn had
All tymys to do chewalry,
With all his rout in full gret hy
Folowyt the traiss quhar gane war thai,
And befor midmorne off the day
The myst wox cler all sodanly.
And than he and his cumpany
War nocht a bowdrawcht fra the rout.
Than schot thai on thaim with a schout.
For gyff thai fled thai wyst that thai
Suld nocht weill feyrd[2] part get away.   [2] fourth.
Tharfor in awentur to dey
He wald him put or[3] he wald fley.   [3] ere.
And quhen the Inglis cumpany
Saw on thaim cum sa sodanly
Sik folk, for-owtyn abaysyng[4],   [4] Such folk with-
Thai war stonayt for effraying[5].   out abashment.
And the tothyr, but mar abaid[6],   [5] terror.
Swa hardely amang thaim raid   [6] without more
That fele off thaim till erd thai bar.   delay.
Stonayit sa gretly than thai war
Throw the force off that fyrst assay
That thai war in-till gret effray;

And wend[1] befor thai had bene ma,
For that thai war assailit swa.
Quhen thai had thyrlyt[2] thaim hastily
Than Schyr Eduuardis cumpany
Set stoutly in the heid[3] agayne.
And at that courss borne doune and slayn
War off thair fayis a gret party,
That thai effrayit war sa gretly
That thai war scalyt[4] gretly then.
And quhen Schyr Eduuard and his men
Saw thaim in-till sa ewill aray
The thrid tyme on thaim prekyt[5] thai.
And thai that saw thaim sa stoutly
Come on, dred thaim sa gretumly
That all thar rowt, bath less and mar,
Fled prekand, scalyt[6] her and thar.
Wes nane amang thaim sa hardy
To bid; bot all comonaly
Fled to warand[7]; and he gan chass
That wilfull to destroy thaim was.
And sum he tuk, and sum war slayn;
Bot Schyr Amery with mekill payn
Eschapyt, and his gat is gayn[8].
His men discumfyt war ilkane;
Sum tane, sum slayne, sum gat away.
It wes a rycht fayr poynt perfay[9].

[1] supposed.

[2] ridden through.

[3] Charged headlong.

[4] dispersed.

[5] spurred.

[6] scattered.

[7] shelter.

[8] went his way.

[9] right proper point of war indeed.

Thomas Randolph

[Douglas coming one night to a house on the Water of Lynn
listens and hears someone inside say, " The devil !" Judging
his enemies to be within he surrounds the house, and after a
fierce fight secures several notable prisoners, among others
Bruce's nephew, Randolph, and his own cousin, Alexander
Stewart.]

That nycht the gud lord off Dowglas
Maid to Schyr Alysander, that was
His emyss[1] sone, rycht glaidsome cher.
Swa did he als, with-owtyn wer[2],
Till Thomas Randell; for that he
Wes to the king in ner degre
Off blud, for his sistre him bar.
And on the morne, for-owtyn mar[3],
Towart the noble king he raid,
And with him bath thai twa he haid.
The king off his present was blyth,
And thankyt him weill fele syth[4].
And till hys nevo gan he say
" Thou has ane quhill renyid thi fay[5],
Bot thou reconsalit now mon be."
Then till the king ansueryt he,
And said, ' Ye chasty[6] me; bot ye
Aucht bettre chastyt for to be.
For sene ye werrayit[7] the king
Off Ingland, in playne fechting[8]
Ye suld press to derenyhe[9] [your] rycht,
And nocht with cowardy na with slycht.'
The king said, " Yeit fall it may
Cum, or oucht lang[10], to sic assay.

[1] uncle's.

[2] without restriction, *lit.* guard.

[3] without more (ado).

[4] very many times.

[5] forsworn thy allegiance.

[6] reprove.

[7] made war on.

[8] in open fight.

[9] determine by battle.

[10] erelong.

Bot sen thow spekys sa rudly,

1 reason.

It is gret skyll¹ men chasty

Thai proud wordis till that thow knaw

2 bend to it as thou ought.

The rycht, and bow it as thow aw²."

The king, for-owtyn mar delaying,

Send him to be in ferme keping

Quhar that he allane suld be

3 effort.

Nocht all apon his powsté³ fre.

And quhen a litill time wes went,

Eftre Thomas Randell he sent;

And sa weile with him tretit he,

4 engaged.

That he his man hecht⁴ for to be.

And the king his ire him forgave:

5 heighten.

And for to hey⁵ his state him gave

Murreff, and erle tharoff him maid,

And othyr sundry landis braid

He gave him in-till heretage.

6 valorous achievement.

He knew his worthi wasselage⁶

7 his sagacity and his prudence.

And his gret wit and his awyss⁷,

His traist hart, and his lele seruice.

8 he put faith.

Tharfor in him affyit he⁸,

And ryche maid him off land and fe,

As it wes certis rycht worthi.

For, and men spek off him trewly,

He wes swa curageous ane knycht,

Sa wyss, sa worthy, and sa wycht,

9 goodness.

And off sa souerane gret bounté⁹,

10 much.

That mekill¹⁰ off him may spokyn be.

11 discourse.

And for I think off him to rede¹¹,

And to schaw part off his gud dede,
I will discryve now his fassoun[1]
And part off his condicioun.
He wes off mesurabill statur[2],
And weile porturat at mesur[3],
With braid wesage, plesand and fayr,
Curtaiss at poynt, and debonayr,
And off rycht sekyr contenyng[4].
Lawté he lowyt atour[5] all thing;
Falset, tresoun, and felony,
He stud agayne ay encrely[6].
He heyit[7] honour ay, and larges[8],
And ay mantemyt[9] rychtwysnes.
In cumpany solacious[10]
He was, and tharwith amorous.
And gud knychtis he luffyt ay.
And, giff I the suth sall say,
He wes fulfillit off bounté,
Als off wertuys all maid was he.
I will commend him her no mar:
Bot ye sall her weile forthyrmar
That he for his dedis worthy
Suld weile be prysyt souerandly[11].

Quhen the king thus was with him saucht[12],
And gret lordschippis had him betaucht[13],
He woux sa wyse and sa awysé
That his land fyrst weill stablyst he,
And syne he sped him to the wer,
Till help his eyme in his myster[14].

[1] describe the fashion of him.
[2] middle stature.
[3] showed his height well.
firm demeanour.
[5] Truth he esteemed above.
[6] in his heart.
[7] exalted.
[8] liberty.
[9] possessed.
[10] cheerful.
[11] sovereignly.
[12] softened.
[13] bestowed.
[14] need.

The Battle of Bannockburn.

[Meanwhile the king has routed the forces of John of Lorn under Ben Cruachan, and has taken Dunstaffnage. William Bunnock, a doughty farmer, concealing men under his supplies of hay, has surprised Linlithgow peel. Douglas on St. Fastern's Eve, approaching upon hands and knees in the dusk, has his men mistaken for a herd of wandering cattle, and succeeds in scaling the walls of Roxburgh. And Randolph, after a hopeless siege, gains access to Edinburgh Castle by a perilous lover's path, and wins it for the king. Edward Bruce, having overcome all Galloway and Nithsdale and reduced Rutherglen and Dundee, lays siege to Stirling. The place is impregnable, but at last, provisions running low, the governor offers to make a treaty to deliver the castle provided it be not relieved by midsummer. Edward Bruce agrees. The king at the intelligence blames his brother's rashness in allowing so long a grace to so powerful an enemy, but nevertheless makes the best preparation he can. At the same time Edward II. of England, seeing here an opportunity of conquering the whole of the north at one blow, summons all his resources. A hundred thousand men assemble on the east border. Here Edward joins them, and they are arrayed under renowned leaders.]

Quhen the king apon this kyn wyss[1]
Had ordanyt, as Ik her diuiss,
His bataillis and his stering[2],
He raiss arly in a mornyng,
And fra Berwik he tuk the way.
Bath hillis and walis helyt[3] thai,
As the bataillis that war braid
Departyt our the feldis raid[4].
The sone wes brycht and schynand cler,
And armouris that burnyst wer
Swa blomyt with the sonnys beme
That all the land wes in a leme[5].
Baneris rycht fayrly flawmand[6]
And penselys to the wynd wawand[7]

[1] thus-wise.

[2] governing.

[3] covered.

[4] Rode disposed over the fields.

[5] blaze.

[6] displayed.

[7] streamers waving.

Swa fele thar war of ser quentiss[1]
That it war gret slycht[2] to diuioc.
And suld I tell all thar affer[3],
Thar contenance, and thar maner,
Thoucht I couth I suld combryt be.
The king, with all that gret menye,
Till Edinburgh he raid him rycht.
Thai war all out to fele[4] to fycht
With few folk of a symple land.
Bot quhar God helpys quhat ma withstand?

1 fair design.

2 skill.

3 equipment.

4 too many.

The king Robert, quhen he hard say
That Inglis men in sic aray
And in-to sua gret quantité
Come in his land, in hy gert he
His men be somound generaly.
And thai come all, full wilfully,
To the Torwood, quhar that the king
Had ordanyt to mak thair meting.

[Edward Bruce, Stewart, Douglas, and Randolph join the king, and the Scottish forces number over thirty thousand. Bruce arranges them in four "battles." On Saturday he hears that the English are in Edinburgh. Accordingly he leads his army to the New Park before Stirling, and to equalize the conflict, honeycombs the ground on his left with foot-pits against cavalry. At sunrise on Sunday the Scots hear mass, and that day keep fast for the Vigil of St. John. Bruce bids all who are faint-hearted leave the field, but all answer with a cry of resolution. That night the English lie at Falkirk, and Murray is set to keep succours out of Stirling. Next day the English appear, covering hill and plain with shining mail and waving banners. They detach eight hundred horse under Clifford to relieve Stirling by making a circuit. The king pointing this out to Murray declares that "a rose of his chaplet is fallen." The latter, stung and mortified, dashes against the succours with five hundred men, and after a terrible conflict puts them to rout. Meanwhile the main body of the English approaches.]

And quhen the king wist that thai wer,
In hale bataill, cummand sa ner,
His bataill gert he weill array.
He raid apon a litill palfray,
Laucht[1], and joly arayand
His bataill, with an ax in hand.
And on his bassynet he bar
An hat of tyre aboune ay quhar[2],
And thar-wpon, in-to taknyng[3],
Ane hey croune, that he wes king.

And quhen Glosyster and Herfurd war
With thair bataill approchand ner,
Befor thaim all thar come rydand,
With helm on heid and sper in hand,
Schyr Henry the Boune, the worthi,
That wes a wycht knycht, and a hardy,
And to the erle off Herfurd cusyne,
Armyt in armys gud and fyne,
Come on a sted a bow-schote ner,
Befor all othyr that thar wer;
And knew the king, for that he saw
Him swa rang his men on raw[4],
And by the croune that wes set
Alsua apon his bassynet.
And towart him he went in hy[5].
And [quhen] the king sua apertly[6]
Saw him cum forouth all his feris[7],
In hy till him the hors he steris[8].
And quhen Schyr Henry saw the king
Cum on, for-owtyn abaysing,

[1] clad (in mail).

[2] a tiara hat above everything.
[3] in token.

[4] range in row.

[5] haste.
[6] boldly.
[7] before his comrades.
[8] steers.

Till him he raid in full gret hy.
He thoucht that he suld weill lychtly[1]
Wyn[2] him and haf him at his will,
Sen he him horsyt saw sa ill.
Sprent thai samyn in-till a ling[3].
Schyr Henry myssit the noble king;
And he, that in his sterapys stud,
With the ax that wes hard and gud
With sa gret mayne raucht him a dynt[4]
That nothyr hat na helm mycht stynt[5]
The hewy dusche[6] that he him gave,
That ner the heid till the harnys[7] clave.
The hand ax schaft fruschit in twa[8],
And he doune to the erd gan ga
All flatlynys, for him faillyt mycht.
This wes the fyrst strak off the fycht.

[1] very easily.
[2] reach.
[3] They sped together in a line.
[4] With so great strength reached him a blow.
[5] stop.
[6] heavy crash.
[7] brain.
[8] shivered in two.

[As night falls Bruce addresses his troops, orders their conduct on the morrow, and declares their enemies already morally discomfited. Next morning he makes knights and arrays his battle.]

And quhen the king off Ingland
Swa the Scottis saw tak on hand,
Takand the hard feyld sa opynly,
And apon fute, he had ferly[9],
And said, "Quhat! will yone Scottis fycht?"
'Ya sekyrly!' said a knycht,
Schyr Ingrame the Wmfrawill hat he[10];
And said, 'Forsuth now, Schyr, I se
It is the mast ferlyfull sycht
That euyre I saw, quhen for to fycht
The Scottis men has tane on hand

[9] he marvelled.
[10] he was called.

Agayne the mycht of Ingland
In plane hard feild to giff bataile.
Bot, and ye will trow[1] my consaill,
Ye sall discomfyt thaim lychtly.
Withdrawys you hyne[2] sodandly,
With bataillis and with penownys,
Quhill that we pass our pailyownyis[3];
And ye sall se alsone that thai,
Magre[4] thair lordys, sall brek aray
And scaile[5] thaim our harnays[6] to ta.
And quhen we se thaim scalit sua
Prik we than on thaim hardely,
And we sall haf thaim wele lychtly:
For than sall nane be knyt[7] to fycht
That may withstand your mekill mycht.'
"I will nocht," said the king, "perfay,
Do sa: for thar sall na man say
That I sall eschew the bataill,
Na withdraw me for sic rangaile[8]."

Quhen this wes said, that er said I,
The Scottis men comounaly
Knelyt all doune, to God to pray.
And a schort prayer thar maid thai
To God, to help thaim in that fycht.
And quhen the Inglis king had sycht
Off thaim kneland, he said in hy,
"Yone folk knel to ask mercy."
Schyr Ingrahame said, 'Ye say suth now.
Thai ask mercy; bot nane at yow.
For thair trespas to God thai cry.

[1] trust.
[2] hence.
[3] pavilions.
[4] despite.
[5] scatter.
[6] furnishing.
[7] embodied.
[8] rabble.

I tell yow a thing sekyrly,
That yone men will all wyn or de:
For doute of dede[1] thai sall nocht fle.'   [1] fear of death.
"Now be it sa than," said the king.
And than, but langer delaying,
Thai gert trump till the assemblé[2].   [2] joining of battle.
On athir sid men mycht than se
Mony a wycht man and worthi
Redy to do chewalry.

[The divisions of Edward Bruce, Murray, and Douglas each
are attacked. The king, observing how the English archers
gall his troops, despatches Sir Robert Keith with five hundred
light horse, who destroys and routs them utterly. Meanwhile
the Scottish archers make havoc among the English cavalry.]

And the gud king Robert, that ay
Wes fillyt off full gret bounté,
Saw how that his bataillis thre
Sa hardely assemblyt thar
And sa weill in the fycht thaim bar,
And swa fast on thair fayis gan ding[3]   [3] drive.
That him thoucht nane had abaysing,
And how the archeris war scalyt then,
He was all blyth; and till his men
He said, "Lordingis, now luk that ye
Worthy and off gud cowyn[4] be   [4] artifice, conduct.
At thys assemblé, and hardy,
And assembill sa sturdely
That na thing may befor yow stand.
Our men are sa freschly fechtand
That thai thair fayis has grathyt sua[5]   [5] prepared so.

That be thai pressyt, Ik wndreta[1],
A litill fastyr, ye sal se
That thai discumfyt sone sall be."

Quhen this wes said thai held thair way,
And on ane feld assemblyt thai
Sa stoutly, that at thair cummyng
Thair fayis war ruschyt a gret thing[2].
Thar mycht men se men felly[3] fycht,
And men that worthi war and wycht
Do mony worthi wasselage[4].
Thai faucht as thai war in a rage;
For quhen the Scottis archery
Saw thair fayis sa sturdely
Stand in-to bataill thaim agayn,
With all thair mycht and all thair mayn
Thai layid on, as men out of wit,
And quhar thai with full strak mycht hyt,
Thar mycht na armur stynt thair strak.
Thai to fruchyt[5] that thai mycht our-tak,
And with axys sic duschys gave
That thai helmys and hedis clave.
And thar fayis rycht hardely
Met thaim, and dang on thaim douchtely,
With wapnys that war styth of stele[6].
Thar wes the bataill strekyt wele[7].
Sa gret dyn thar wes of dyntis,
As wapnys apon armur styntis,
And off speris sa gret bresting[8],
And sic thrang[9], and sic thrysting,
Sic gyrnyng[10], granying[11], and sa gret

2 driven (back) a great deal.
3 fiercely.

4 achievements.

5 also broke (rank).

6 weapons strong of steel.
7 engaged in well.

8 breaking.
9 rushing together.
10 grinning.
11 groaning.

A noyis, as thai gan othyr beit,
And ensenyeys[1] on ilka sid,
Gewand and takand woundis wid,
That it wes hydwyss for to her.

[1] war-cries.

All thair four bataillis with that wer
Fechtand in a frount halyly.
A mychty God! how douchtely
Schyr Eduuard the Bruce and his men
Amang thair fayis contenyt thaim then!
Fechtand in sa gud covyn,
Sa hardy, worthy, and sa fyne,
That thar waward ruschyt was[2],
And, maugre tharis, left the place,
And till thar gret rout to warand
Thai went; that tane had apon hand
Sa gret anoy that thai war effrayit
For Scottis that thaim hard assayit[3]
That than war in a schiltrum[4] all.
Quha hapnyt in-to that fycht to fall
I trow agane he suld nocht ryss.
Thar mycht men se on mony wyss
Hardimentis eschewyt[5] douchtely,
And mony that wycht war and hardy
Sone liand wndre fete all dede,
Quhar all the feld off blud wes rede.
Armys and quhytyss[6] that thai bar
With blud war sa defoulyt thar
That thai mycht nocht descroyit[7] be.
A mychty God! quha than mycht se
That Stewart, Waltre, and his rout,

[2] their vanguard was driven (back).

[3] attacked.

[4] a host in round formation.

[5] daring deeds achieved.

[6] military hats.

[7] described.

And the gud Douglas that wes sa stout,
Fechtand in-to that stalwart stour,
He suld say that till all honour
Thai war worthi that in that fycht
Sa fast pressyt thair fayis mycht,
That thaim ruschyt quhar thai yeid.
Thar men mycht se mony a steid
Fleand on stray, that lord had nane.
A Lord! quha then gud tent[1] had tane
Till the gud erle of Murreff,
And his, that sa gret rowtis geff[2],
And faucht sa fast in that battaill,
Tholand[3] sic paynys and trawaill
That thai and tharis maid sic debat[4]
That quhar thai come thai maid thaim gat.
Than mycht men her enseynyeis cry,
And Scottis men cry hardely,
"On thaim! On thaim! On thaim! Thai faile!"
With that sa hard thai gan assaile,
And slew all that thai mycht our-ta,
And the Scottis archeris alsua
Schot amang them sa deliuerly,
Engrewand[5] thaim sa gretumly,
That quhat for thaim that with thaim faucht
That swa gret rowtis to thaim raucht
And pressyt thaim full egrely,
And quhat for arowis that felly[6]
Mony gret woundis gan thaim ma
And slew fast off thair horss alsua,
That thai wandyst a litill wei[7].
Thai dred sa gretly then to dey

[1] attention.

[2] so great blows gave.

[3] undergoing.

[4] contention.

[5] vexing.

[6] in dire manner.

[7] showed fear somewhat.

That thair cowyn wes wer and wer[1].

For thai that fechtand with thaim wer

Set hardement and strenth and will

And hart and corage als thar-till,

And all thair mayne and all thair mycht,

To put thaim fully to [the] flycht.

[1] their carriage was worse and worse.

[At this point the Scottish camp-followers, who had been ordered to the rear by Bruce, desiring to see the battle, mount sheets on poles for banners, and, fifteen thousand strong, are seen coming over the Gillies' Hill. The distant sight utterly disheartens the wearied English, who take it for the approach of fresh Scottish reserves. As Bruce leads a new attack in person they begin to give way, and the rout is soon general.]

And quhen the king of Ingland

Saw his men fley in syndry place,

And saw his fayis rout that was

Worthyn[2] sa wycht and sa hardy—

That all his folk war halyly

Sa stonayit[3] that thai had na mycht

To stynt[4] thair fayis in the fycht—

He was abaysyt[5] sa gretumly

That he and his cumpany,

Fyve hundre, armyt all at rycht,

In-till a frusch[6] all tok the flycht,

And to the castell held thair way.

And yeyt haiff Ik hard som men say

That of Walence Schir Aymer,

When he the feld saw wencusyt ner,

Be the reyngye led away the king,

Agayne his will, fra the fechting.

[2] become.

[3] dismayed.

[4] stay.

[5] confounded.

[6] broken rout.

And quhen Schyr Gylis the Argenté

Saw the king thus and his menye

Schap thaim to fley sa spedyly,

He come rycht to the king in hy

And said, "Schyr, sen it is sua

That ye thusgat your gat will ga[1],

Hawys gud day! for agayne will I.

Yeyt fled I neuir sekyrly[2],

And I cheyss her to bid[3] and dey,

Than for to lyve schamly, and fley."

Hys bridill, but mar abad,

He turnyt, and agayne he rade,

And on Eduuard the Bruyss rout,

That wes sa sturdy and sa stout

As drede off nakyn[4] thing had he,

He prikyt, cryand, "The Argenté!"

And thai with spuris swa him met,

And swa fele[5] speris on him set,

That he and hors war chargyt swa

That bathe till the erd gan ga,

And in that place thar slane wes he.

Off hys deid wes rycht gret pité;

He wes the thrid best knycht, perfay,

That men wyst lywand[6] in his day.

[Thirty thousand dead and all the English baggage are left on the field. Douglas pursues King Edward to Dunbar, and night falls upon the weary but joyful army of Scotland.]

And on the morn quhen day wes lycht

The king raiss, as his willis[7] was.

Than ane Inglis knycht, throw cass[8],

Hapnyt that he yeid wawerand[9],

Swa that na man laid on him hand.

In a busk[10] he hid hys armyng,

[1] thus your way will go.

[2] assuredly.

[3] choose here to abide.

[4] no kind of.

[5] many.

[6] knew living.

[7] custom.

[8] by chance.

[9] wandering, *lit.* wavering.

[10] bush.

And waytyt quhill he saw the king
In the morne cum forth arly:
Till him than is he went in hy
Schyr Marmeduk the Twengue he hycht[1].

[1] was named.

He raykyt[2] till the king all rycht,

[2] reached, *lit.* ranged.

And halyst[3] him upon his kne.

[3] saluted.

"Welcum, Schyr Marmeduk," said he;
"To quhat man art thow presoner?"
'To nane,' he said, 'bot to you her.
I yeld me at your will to be.'
"And I ressave the, Schyr," said he.
Than gert[4] he tret him curtasly.

[4] caused.

He duelt lang in his cumpany,
And syne till Ingland him send he,
Arayit weile, but ransoun fre,
And geff him gret gyftis tharto.
A worthi man that sua wald do
Mycht mak him gretly for to prise[5].

[5] be praised.

Quhen Marmeduk apon this wiss
Was yoldyn[6], as Ik to yow say,

[6] yielded.

Than come Schir Philip the Mowbray
And to the king yauld the castell.
His cunnand hes he haldyn[7] well,

[7] his covenant has he kept.

And with him tretyt sua the king,
That he belewyt[8] of his duelling,

[8] delivered up.

And held him lelely his fay
Quhill the last end off his lyf day.

[Among the results of the battle Bruce receives back his queen and his daughter Marjory in exchange for the Earl of Hereford. Marjory is married to Walter Stewart, and the king sets his realm in order.]

The King and the Lavyndar.

[After the battle of Bannockburn the poem proceeds to recount the enterprises and successes of the king's generals. While Douglas holds the Border, Edward Bruce carries victory into Ireland. King Robert himself during one campaign takes the command there, and during their march then a point of chivalry is noticed.]

The king has hard a woman cry;
He askyt quhat that wes in hy[1].
" It is the layndar[2], Schyr," said ane,
" That hyr child-ill[3] rycht now has tane,
And mon[4] leve now behind ws her :
Tharfor scho makys yone iwill[5] cher."
The king said, ' Certis, it war pité
That scho in that poynt[6] left suld be ;
For certis I trow thar is na man
That he ne will rew a woman than.'
Hiss ost all thar arestyt he,
And gert a tent sone stentit[7] be,
And gert hyr gang[8] in hastily,
And othyr wemen to be hyr by.
Quhill scho wes deliuer he bad,
And syne furth on his wayis raid.
And how scho furth suld caryit be,
Or euir he furth fur[9], ordanyt he.
This wes a full gret curtasy,
That swilk[10] a king, and sa mychty,
Gert his men duell on this maner,
Bot for a pouir lauender.

1 in haste.
2 laundress.
3 travail-pains.
4 must.
5 evil.
6 extremity.
7 set up.
8 go.
9 fared forth.
10 such.

The Death of Bruce.

[Berwick, the last stronghold in Scotland held by the English, is taken by Douglas and Randolph, and Walter Stewart installed as governor. Then follows a long, minute, and stirring account of its siege by the English king. Bruce finally relieves the place by making a counter-march into England which draws off the besiegers. In Ireland Edward Bruce is slain at last in a rash attack against hopeless odds, and that country in consequence is presently abandoned to its English holders. Encouraged by this event, Edward II. makes one more attempt upon Scotland with his whole force. But Bruce burns and drives all forage into the north, and the English army, finding neither enemy to fight nor provisions to eat, is compelled to retire. It is followed by Bruce, and finally at Biland, in Yorkshire, is in its famished state put to utter rout. King Robert next devotes himself to the establishment of justice and order in his kingdom, concludes and enforces a peace with England, and after, with the consent of his parliament, settling the succession first on his son, and, failing him, on the children of his daughter Marjory and Walter Stewart, dies in ease and honour at Cardross on the Clyde.]

Quhen all this thing thus tretit wes
And affermyt with sekyrnes[1],   [1] confirmed securely.
The king to Cardros went in hy,
And thar him tuk sa fellely[2]   [2] severely.
The seknes, and him trawailit swa,
That he wyst him behowyt to ma
Off all his liff the commoun end,
That is to dede, quhen God will send.
Tharfor his lettrys sone send he
For the lordis off his countré,
And thai come as thai biddyng had.
His testament than has he maid
Befor bath lordis and prelatis;
And to religioun of ser statis[3]   [3] several establishments.
For hele of his saule gaf he
Siluer into gret quantité.

He ordanyt for his saule weill,
And quhen this done wes ilkadele[1]
He said, " Lordingis, swa is it gayn
With me that thar is nocht bot ane,
That is the dede, withowtyn drede,
That ilk man mon thole off nede.
And I thank God that has me sent
Space in this lyve me to repent;
For throwch me and my werraying[2]
Off blud has bene rycht gret spilling,
Quhar mony sakles[3] men war slayn.
Tharfor this seknes and this payn
I tak in thank for my trespass.
And myn hart fichyt[4] sekirly was
Quhen I wes in prosperité,
Off my synnys to sauffyt[5] be
To trawaill apon Goddis fayis.
And sen he now me till him tayis[6],
Swa that the body may na-wyss
Fullfill that the hart gan dewyss[7],
I wald the hart war thiddyr sent
Quhar-in consawyt[8] wes that entent.
Tharfor I pray yow euirilkan[9]
That ye amang yow chess me ane
That be honest, wiss, and wicht,
And off his hand a noble knycht,
On Goddis fayis my hart to ber
Quhen saule and corss disseueryt er.
For I wald it war worthily
Broucht thar, sen God will nocht that I
Haiff pouer thiddyrwart to ga."

1 every whit.

2 war-making.

3 blameless.

4 fixed.

5 absolved.

6 takes.

7 devise.

8 conceived.

9 everyone.

Than war thair hartis all sar wa[1]
That nayne mycht hald him fra greting[2].
He bad thaim leve thair sorowing;
For it, he said, mycht nocht releve,
And mycht thaim rycht gretly engreve[3];
And prayit thaim in hy to do
The thing that thai war chargit to.
Than went thai furth with drery mode.
Amang thaim thai thocht it gode
That the worthi lord of Douglas
Best schapyn for that trawaill was.
And quhen the king hard that thai swa
Had ordanyt him his hart to ta
That he mast yarnyt suld it haff,
He said, "Sa God him-self me saiff!
I hald me rycht weill payit that yhe
Haff chosyn him; for his bounté
And his worschip set my yarnyng
Ay sen I thoucht to do this thing,
That he it with him thar suld ber.
And sen ye all assentit er
It is the mar likand[4] to me.
Lat se now quhat thar-till sayis he."
And quhen the gud lord of Douglas
Wist that thing thus spokyn was
He come and knelit to the king,
And on this wiss maid him thanking.
"I thank you gretly, lord," said he,
"Off mony largess and gret bounté
That yhe haff done me felsyss[5]
Sen fyrst I come to your seruice.

[1] sorely woful.
[2] weeping.

[3] vex.

[4] agreeable.

[5] very often.

Bot our all thing I mak thanking
That ye sa dyng[1] and worthi thing
As your hart that enlumynt wes
Of all bounté and all prowes
Will that I in my yemsall[2] tak.
For yow, Schyr, I will blythly mak
This trawaill, gif God will me gif
Layser and space swa lang to lyff."
The king him thankyt tendrely.
Than wes nane in that cumpany
That thai na wepyt for pité.
Thar cher anoyus wes to se.

Quhen the Lord Douglas on this wiss
Had wndretane sa hey empriss[3]
As the gud kyngis hart to ber
On Goddis fayis apon wer
Prissyt for his empriss wes he.
And the kingis infirmyté
Woux mar and mar, quhill at the last
The dulfull dede approchit fast.
And quhen he had gert till him do
All that gud crystyn man fell to
With werray[4] repentance he gaf
The gast, that God till hewyn haiff
Amang his chossyn folk to be
In joy, solace, and angell gle !
And fra his folk wyst he wes ded
The sorow raiss fra steid to steid[5].
Thar mycht men se men ryve[6] thair har,
And comounly kychtis gret full sar[7],

And thar newffys[1] oft samyn[2] dryve,

And as woud[3] men thair clathis ryve,

Regratand his worthi bounté,

His wyt, his strenth, his honesté;

And our all, the gret cumpany

That he thaim maid oft curtasly.

"All our defens," thai said, "allace!

And he that all our comford was,

Our wyt and all our gouernyng,

Allace! is brought her till ending!

His worschip and his mekill[4] mycht

Maid all that war with him sa wycht[5]

That thai mycht neuir abaysit be

Quhill forouth[6] thaim thai mycht him se.

Allace! quhat sall we do or say?

For on lyff quhill he lestyt, ay

With all our nychtbowris dred war we,

And in-till mony ser countré

Off our worschip sprang the renoun;

And that wes all for his persoune."

With swilk[7] wordis thai maid thair mayn;

And sekyrly woundre wes nane[8],

For better gouernour than he

Mycht in na countré fundyn be.

[1] hands.
[2] together.
[3] mad.
[4] great.
[5] able.
[6] in front of.
[7] such.
[8] assuredly it was no wonder.

[The poem ends with the death of Douglas in his attempt to carry the Bruce's heart through Spain to the Holy Land. Successful in a great battle against the Saracens, the Scottish company presses the pursuit too far, and some of the knights are presently surrounded. Perceiving Sir William St. Clair battling against hopeless odds, Douglas exclaims, "Yonder brave knight will be slain if he have not help," and spurring again into the fray he falls there with his friends. The king's heart is brought home again, and buried by Murray in Melrose Abbey.]

ANDROW OF WYNTOUN.

ANDROW OF WYNTOUN.

THERE have been chroniclers and there have been historians, and the office of the one is not to be mistaken for the office of the other. The chronicler undertakes to do no more than set down in the order of their happening the events and circumstances of a certain time. The object of the historian, on the other hand, is to sift and and assort facts, to show their relation, and by their proper arrangement and interpretation to reveal the principles of their occurrence, the tragedy and comedy which everywhere underlie the outer movement of events. Androw of Wyntoun made no claim to the title of historian. He called his work simply a chronicle of Scotland, and it does not appear that he aimed at greater things than the name suggests. It may be said that the opportunity lay to his hand, as an ecclesiastic familiar with the sources of information, to write a great epic of the Scottish Church, displaying behind the events of history that church's rise to power among the estates of the realm. He did not, however, essay the laurels of the epic poet. Other ideals of poetry, moreover, probably formed as small a part of his

object. As he did not attempt any masterly grouping
of the march of events towards a national purpose, so,
it would seem, he had no thought of touching with
artistic design the plain circumstances of his narrative.
The reader will look through the *Cronykil of Scotland*
almost in vain for the excitement of a dramatic
situation, the contrast and climax of human emotion.
Hardly at all will he find that focussing of objects to
their most interesting point of view which dis-
tinguishes a picture from a map, the work of the
artist from the work of the artizan.   Nowhere, it may
safely be said, will he taste the breath of that ethereal
wine, strangely stirring the heart, which is the vintage
of great poetic genius.

The chief value of Wyntoun's work must remain its
value as a chronicle, its worth as material for history.
In this respect its importance has long been
recógnised, and out of its substance, by craftsmen
like Tytler, Scott, and Hill Burton, have been quarried
the corner-stones of many a historic edifice.   As
material for poetry, however, if not always as poetry
itself, the *Cronykil* is deserving of more attention than
it has yet received.   Many of the circumstances of
the remote period set forth in its pages have a quaint
picturesqueness peculiar to themselves.   Wyntoun
had a happy faculty for collecting and incorporating
typical facts and stories ; and amid the huge mass of
his narrative, neglected mostly because of the labour
of finding them, there are discoverable glimpses of
scenes and episodes set in a romantic atmosphere
without conscious effort of art.   For the fair

preservation of these, rather than for the poor fact of his work being presented in form of rhythm, the author of the *Orygynale Cronykil* must maintain a place of respect among the early poets of Scotland.

Almost all that is known of Wyntoun himself has been gathered from the pages of his work. Regarding his origin nothing whatever has been discovered, and even with the aid of his own occasional references his personality comes but dimly out of the cloister dusk of the past. His chronicle is supposed to have been finished between 1419 and 1424, as it mentions the death of Robert, Duke of Albany, which occurred at the former date, but says nothing of the return of James I. from captivity, which took place in the latter year. Probably he did not long survive the completion of his work. In the prologue to the last book he declares himself an aged man :

> Off this Tretys the last end
> Tyl bettyr than I am I commend ;
> For, as I stabil myne intent,
> Offt I fynd impediment
> Wyth sudane and fers maladis
> That me cumbris mony wis,
> And elde me mastreis wyth hir brevis,
> Ilke day me sare aggrevis.
> Scho has me maid monitioune
> To se for a conclusioune
> The quhilk behovis to be of det.
> Quhat term of tyme of that be set
> I can wyt it be na way ;
> Bot, weil I wate, on schorte delay
> At a court I mon appeire
> Fell accusationis thare til here,
> Quhare na help thare is bot grace.

In the chartulary of St. Andrew's as early as 1395,
at a perambulation held " in presentia serenissimi
principis Roberti Ducis Albanie," Wyntoun is men-
tioned as Prior of the island in Loch Leven; and as
he must have been of mature years before obtaining
this position his birth has been set about the middle
of the reign of David II., say about 1350.

In the prologue to the *Cronykil* he describes
himself:

> And, for I wyll nane bere the blame
> Off my defawte, [this] is my name
> Be baptysyne, ANDROWE OF WYNTOUNE,
> Off Sanctandrowys a Chanowne
> Regulare, bot noucht-for-thi
> Off thaim all the lest worthy;
> Bot off thare grace and thaire faẅoure
> I wes, but meryt, made Priowre
> Off the Ynche wythin Lochleẅyne,
> Haẅand tharof my tytill eẅyne
> Off Sanctandrowys dyocesy,
> Betwene the Lomownde and Bennarty.

Notwithstanding his modest denial of merit it may be
understood that Androw of Wyntoun, as an
ecclesiastic, was likely to be a man of no mean
powers.   The prior of an ancient monastery, who
was also a canon regular of the metropolitan see of
St. Andrew's, could hardly be an altogether insignifi-
cant person.   The Church in Scotland, owning, it is
said, from a third to a half of the whole lands of the
country, was then approaching the height of her
political power, and the dignities of St. Andrew's See
were prizes sought after by the best blood and the
most ambitious in the realm.   Five sub-priories

belonged to St. Andrew's : Monymusk in Aberdeen-shire, the Isle of May in the Firth of Forth, Pittenweem in Fife, and Portmoak and St. Serf's in Kinross. The last-named religious house, situated on the inch or island in Lochleven, was said to have been a Culdee monastery founded by Brud, king of the Picts, about the year 700. In this still, romantic spot Wyntoun must have spent many of the riper years of his life; and here, with little to break the quiet of the hours but the lapse of waves on the islet beach and the sweet chime at intervals of the monastery bells, it is probable he wrote the pages of his book.

A few years earlier John of Fordun, a chantry priest of the cathedral of Aberdeen, had written in Latin his chronicle of the Scottish nation, afterwards amplified by Bower, who died abbot of Inch Colme, into the work now known as the *Scoti-chronicon.* But it is certain that Wyntoun never saw this work, and when the suggestion of writing a narrative of national events was made to him he quietly set about the task of independent research and original composition in the vernacular.

The inception of the work is owed to an ancestor of the noble family of Wemyss.

> This trelys sympylly
> I made at the instans of a larde
> That hade my serŵys in his warde,
> Schyr Jhone of the Wemys be rycht name,
> An honest knycht and of gude fame.

As it stands, the *Cronykil* is the earliest composition of strictly historical purpose extant in the vernacular of the north, and, strangely enough, for fully two hundred years afterwards, excepting the translations of Ballenden and Read, no other history of the Scottish people was written in the Scottish tongue. A considerable number of manuscripts of the work are in existence. The best of them is the Royal MS. in the British Museum, a transcript made for George Barclay of Achrody probably not later than 1430. From this, collated with MSS. of the Cotton, Harleian, and Advocates' libraries, the first printed edition was made by David Macpherson in 1795. In that edition, upon the principle of excluding all that did not immediately belong to the history of Scotland, nearly the whole of the first five books of the *Cronykil* were omitted. In 1872-79 another excellent edition by Mr. David Laing, including these books, was printed at Edinburgh in three portly volumes as part of a series of the historians of Scotland. Both of these editions are now somewhat difficult to procure.

Wyntoun called his work *The Orygynale Cronykil of Scotland,* that is, as he explained in his prologue, a chronicle narrating events from the first beginning of things. Accordingly, in the orthodox fashion of his time, he begins with the Creation, and the greater part of the first five books is occupied with the long descent through sacred and profane history. It is only at the beginning of the sixth book that the author settles down to his more immediate subject. The narrative is divided into nine books of very unequal length.

> In honowre of the Ordrys nyne
> Off haly Angelys.

Each book is introduced by a prologue and a
summary of chapters, and each chapter has a rhyming
title, as

> This next folowand Chaptere says
> Quhat done wes in second Robertis days.

Extraordinary care is taken to mention at least the
year of each event. A great part of the *Cronykil*,
indeed, is the merest recording of names and occur-
rences and their dates, and in spite of all the ingenious
variety of the rhymes the reader is apt to grow weary
of bare statements of fact beginning

> A thousand aucht and fourty yhere
> Fra the byrth of our Lord dere,

or

> A thousand, a hundyr, thretty and nyne
> Yheris fra the swete Wyrgyne
> Had borne hyr Sowne.

This characteristic, however valuable from the histori-
cal point of view, seriously interferes with pretensions
to poetic charm. So anxious was Wyntoun to be
authentic that he has actually introduced two speeches
in plain prose, one of them being the declaration of
Henry IV. on assuming the English crown after the
deposition of Richard II. On the other hand, he
shared the easy habit of the chroniclers of his age, such
as Robert of Gloucester and Robert of Brunne, of
omitting such portions of history as were already
known to be written by other hands. For this reason
he omits the history of Alexander the Great, the wars
of the Saxons and Britons, the actions of Wallace and
Bruce, and the origin of the Stewarts.

The vanity of poetic authorship seems to have influenced him but little, for, besides alluding to his contemporary Barbour again and again in the most self-deprecatory terms, he has incorporated in his eighth book, without alteration, some three hundred lines of *The Bruce.* A considerable portion of the *Cronykil* indeed was avowedly not written by himself. He informs the reader that while engaged upon the work he was presented with a narrative written by some unknown person, and finding it entirely suitable for his purpose, he simply inserted it in his manuscript. In this way thirty-six clearly defined chapters, from the birth of David II. to the death of Robert II., are accounted for. To the same liberality of quotation is owed the preservation of a little elegaic song on the death of Alexander III., which Macpherson considered to be contemporary with the event, that is nearly ninety years older than Barbour's work.

For the purposes of the historian, Wyntoun's work has been simply invaluable. For the events of the last fifty years of his narrative, it has to be remembered, he was himself personally an authority; while "it can scarcely be doubted," says Dr. Irving, "that he had access to many important documents which are irretrievably lost." The reliability of the *Cronykl* is discovered wherever it is possible to compare its account with such unquestioned testimony as the *Fœdera Angliæ* and the remains of the *Register of the Priory of St. Andrew's.* In the famous case of the Sutherland succession Lord Hailes made large use of Wyntoun for evidence of ancient Scottish law and

customs of inheritance; and Macpherson declared
that "the compiler of a Scottish peerage might obtain
from Wyntoun more true information concerning the
ancient noble families of Scotland than is to be found
in any work extant."

Before most things else, perhaps, Wyntoun was a
churchman. Loyal to the uttermost to his order, he
takes special delight in recording the acts and deaths
of the prelates of St. Andrew's. He carefully notices
every founding of an abbey; and Alexander I. and
David I. have the warmest commendation from him
for their munificence to the church. Curious glimpses
of the theology of that day are to be had here
and there in his pages. In the fifth book of the
Cronykil, St. Serf, the patron saint of Wyntoun's
priory, holds a long and somewhat scornful interview
with the Devil, in which the fiend, for the confusion of
his interlocutor, propounds questions as to where God
existed before the making of heaven and earth, and
the like. Malcolm IV. also appears after death to a
friend and furnishes information regarding a future
state.

Touches of credulity and superstition of this sort,
natural to the times, do not, however, affect the truth
of the material narrative. Liberal, rather, and open-
minded beyond his age, Wyntoun displays little of the
rude prejudice which was apt to disfigure the patriotic
writing of the time. Only twice does he launch into
invective against the national enemy—upon the cruelty
of Edward I. to the Scots, and upon the seizure in
time of truce of the young Prince James. Perhaps

the fact most significant of the nationality of the
chronicler is that amid all his references and
quotations he does not once mention the works of
Langland, Gower, or Chaucer, all of whom were his
contemporaries, and flourished in his time. Frequently
indeed the reader is tempted to wish that Wyntoun
had indulged a trifle more in the rhetoric of emotional
description.   It is true that the cruel deaths by
starvation of the gallant Sir Alexander Ramsay at
Hermitage and of the gay young Duke of Rothesay at
Falkland might have been dangerous ground just
then to posture upon ; but pictures might have been
made of incidents like the tragic death of Thomas à
Becket on the Cathedral steps at Canterbury, the
momentous fall from the cliff of Alexander III. at
Kinghorn, and the vindication of the freedom of the
North by her sons at the battle of Stirling Bridge.
These afforded room for stirring narrative—for more,
at anyrate, than the bare mention accorded by the
chronicler.

Wyntoun, however, went his own way.   Other
writers, like Boece, have hidden historic truth alto-
gether under their garniture of fancy, and by
contrast the simple plainness of Wyntoun has value
and effect.   In these pages one reads with an interest
not less striking for their simplicity of statement,
passages like those detailing the original story of
Macbeth, the granting of the boon of Macduff, or the
story of the Lady Devorgille and the founding of
Sweetheart Abbey.   Many such episodes, other-
wise unknown or strangely distorted, are found here

in their historic form. Authentic insight, too, is frequently afforded into the manners of those times, as in the narrative of the rough jousting at Berwick and in the episode with which the *Cronykil* concludes, detailing how the Earl of Mar in 1418 passed over to Paris, and there at the sign of "The Tynnyn Plate" kept open house with regal magnificence for twelve weeks. Stripped of all glamour of sentiment, the rudeness and cruelties of the age appear in realistic strength, as when, rather than yield her trust, the brave Lady of Seton sees her hostage son hanged before her eyes. At the same time the ideals of those centuries are sometimes flashed out in a sentence. It is said of David I.:

> The day he wes bath Kyng and Knycht,
> A Mwnk devote he wes the nycht.

The last episode of the *Cronykil*, detailing the adventures of the Earl of Mar abroad, has no vital connection with the body of the narrative. It was probably an after addition to the volume, and may have been written by way of acknowledgment of some political favour. The work really ends with the capture of James I., an event which happened fourteen years before the date of writing. As Macpherson remarked, at that period "it was rather dangerous for truth to tread too close upon the heels of time." The good prior therefore acted with prudence in bringing his narrative when he did to a close.

It is nearly five hundred years since Wyntoun laid

down his pen. During that time, though never popular with the popularity of Barbour and Blind Harry, he has probably never been quite forgotten. His position as a national chronicler accounts to a large extent for this. But the reader who grows familiar with his pages to-day discovers what may perhaps be another reason. He finds himself making the acquaintance, not only of a teller of quaint historic tales, but of a gentle and pious soul.

THE ORYGYNALE CRONYKIL
OF SCOTLAND.

Early Britain.

[The *Cronykil* begins with a narrative of the earliest events of sacred history—the state of angels, the creation, the flood, &c. Then follows a geographical description of the three continents, ending with the British Isles.]

LESSYDE Bretayne beelde[1] sulde be   [1] model.
Off all the ilys in the se,
Quhare flowrys are fele[2] on feldys fayre, [2] many.
Hale[3] off hewe, haylsum off ayre.   [3] Perfect.
Off all corne thare is copy[4] gret,   [4] abundance,
Pese and atys, bere and qwhet;
Bath froyt on tre and fysche in flwde,
And tyll all catale pasture gwde.
Solynus [sayis] in Bretanny
Sum steddys[5] growys sa habowndanly   [5] places.
Off gyrs[6] that sum-tym, bot thair fe[7]   [6] grass.
   [7] cattle.
Fra fwlth off mete refrenyht be[8],   [8] Be restrained
   from over-
   feeding.
Thair fwde sall turne thame to peryle,
To rot, or bryst, or dey sum quhyle.
Thare wylde in wode has welth at wylle;
Thare hyrdys hydys holme and hille;
Thare bewys bowys all for byrtht[9];   [9] branches bend
   with burden,

Bath merle and maweys mellys off myrtht[1]
Thare huntyng is at allkyne dere[2].
And richt gud hawlkyn[3] on rywere;
Off fysche thair is habowndance,
And nedfulle thyng to mannys substance.

Be west Bretane is lyand
All the landys off Irlande,
That is ane land off nobyl ayre,
Off fyrth and felde and flowrys fayre.
Thare nakyn best off wenym[4] may
Lywe or lest atoure[5] a day,
As ask or eddyre, tade or pade[6],
Suppos that thai be thiddyr hade.

The Rise of Macbeth.

[The generations of the world, the events of oriental and classic history, and the due succession of potentates, emperors, and popes are narrated. Among other legends the travels are told of the "King's Stone," or "Stone of Destiny," from Spain, first to Ireland, then to Scone in Scotland, with its oracle:

NI FALLAT FATUM, SCOTI, QUOCUNQUE LOCATUM
INVENIENT LAPIDEM, REGNARE TENENTUR IBIDEM.

The descent of the Scottish kings is traced to Duncan, a somewhat free-living monarch, who is slain by his sister's son at Elgin.]

In this tyme, as yhe herd me tell
Off trewsone[7] that in Ingland fell,
In Scotland nere the lyk cas
Be Makbeth-Fynlayk practykyd was,
Quhen he mwrthrysyde hys awyne eme[8]
Be hope that he had in a dreme

That he sawe quhen he was yhyng
In hows duelland wyth the king,
That fayrly trettyd hym and welle
In all that langyd hym ilke delle[1].
For he wes hys systyr sone
Hys yharnyng all he gert be done[2].

[1] belonged to him every whit.

[2] Caused his desire to be done.

   A nycht he thowcht in hys dreming
That sittand he was besyd the king
At a sete in hwntyng, swa
In-till a leysh had grewhundys twa.
He thowcht quhile he was swa sittand
He sawe thre wemen by gangand[3],
And thai wemen than thowcht he
Thre werd systrys mast lyk to be.
The fyrst he hard say gangand by,
"Lo, yhondyr the Thayne off Crwmbawchty[4]!"
The tothir woman sayd agayne,
"Off Morave yhondyre I se the Thayne."
The thryd than sayd, "I se the Kyng."
All this he herd in his dremyng.
Sone efftyre that in his yhowthad
Off thyr thayndomys he thayne was made;
Syne neyst he thowcht to be kyng
Fra Duncanys dayis had tane endyng.

[3] going.

[4] Cromarty.

   The fantasy thus of his dreme
Movyd hym mast to sla hys eme,
As he dyd all furth in dede,
As befor yhe herd me rede[5];
And Dame Grwok, hys emys wyff,

[5] recount.

Tuk and led wyth hyr hys lyff,
And held hyr bathe hys wyff and qweyne,
As befor than scho had beyne
Till hys eme qwene lyvand
Quhen he wes kyng wyth crowne ryngnand.
For lytyll in honowre than had he
The greys[1] off affynyté.

[1] degrees.

All thus quhen his eme wes dede
He succedyt in his stede,
And sevyntene wyntyr full rignand
As kyng he wes than in-till Scotland.
All hys tyme wes gret plenté
Abowndand bath in land and se.
He wes in justice rycht lawchfull,
And till hys legis all awfull.
Quhen Leo the Tend wes Pape off Rome
As pylgryne to the curt he come,
And in hys almus he sew sylver[2]
Till all pure folk that had myster[3];
And all tyme oysyd[4] he to wyrk
Profytably for Haly Kyrke.

[2] strewed silver.
[3] need.
[4] used.

The Boon of Macduff.

[Macbeth, with all his good works, is a fierce king. Watching the building of his castle of Dunsinane he one day notices a yoke of oxen fail in drawing timber. He asks whose oxen these are, and being informed that they belong to Macduff, the thane of Fife, he threatens to put the thane's own neck into the yoke and make him draw. Macduff flies, first to Kennachy, where his wife keeps the pursuing king in treaty till she sees her husband's boat beyond reach on the firth, then to the English court, where Duncan's sons have found refuge. The eldest two refuse the enterprise, but the third, Malcolm, a natural son, is roused to avenge his father. Blessed by Edward the Confessor, and joined by Siward, Lord of Northumberland, he invades Scotland, reaches Birnam, and vanquishes Macbeth with almost the exact circumstances immortalized by Shakespeare. Macduff, however, is not the slayer of the king, nor have the thane's wife and children been put to death by Macbeth. Afterwards, for his services, Macduff asks of Malcolm three things.]

Qwhen Makbeth-Fynlayk thus wes slane
Off Fyffe Macduff that tyme the Thane
For his trawaille till his bownté
At Malcolme as Kyng askyd thire thre[1].   [1] these three
                                                  (things).
Fyrst, till hys sete fra the awtare[2]   [2] from the altar.
[That he sulde be the kyngis] ledare,
And in that set thare set hym downe
Till tak his coronatyowne
For hym and hys posteryté
Quhen-evyre the kyng suld crownyd be.*
Efftyre that the secownd thyng
Wes that he askyd at the kyng
Till hawe the waward[3] off hys bataylle   [3] vanguard.

* A memorable instance of the exercise of this privilege was the crowning of Robert the Bruce at Scone by the Countess of Buchan in default of her brother, the Earl of Fife.

Quhat-evyr thai ware wald it assaylle;
That he and hys suld haẅe always
Quhen that the kyng suld banare rays.

¹ war.

Or gyff the Thayne off Fyff in were[1]
Or in-till host wyth hys powere
Ware, the waward suld governyd be
Be hym and hys posteryté.
Efftyre this, the thryd askyng
That he askyt at the kyng,

² broil.

Gyve ony be suddane chawdmellé[2]
Hapnyd swa slayne to be
Be ony off the Thaynys kyne
Off Fyff, the kynryk all wyth-in,
Gyve he swa slayne wer gentill-man
Foure and twenty markys than;
For a yhwman twelf markys ay

³ A mulct paid to kinsmen of slain.

The slaare suld for kynbwt[3] pay,
And haẅe full remyssyowne
Fra thine for all that actyowne.
Gyve ony hapnyd hym to sla

⁴ law.

That to that lawch[4] ware bwndyn swa,
Off that priẅylage evyrmare

⁵ Without part.

Partles[5] suld be the slaare.
Off this lawch are thre capytale;
That is the Blak Prest off Weddale,
The Thayne off Fyffe, and the thryd syne
Quha-eẅyre be Lord off Abbyrnethyne.*

* So late as 1421 the Stewart in Fife received three gentlemen who had been concerned in the slaughter of Melvil of Glenbervy to the *Lach of Clan-Macduff*, three of their friends being securities for proof of their kindred to Macduff.—*Macpherson.*

Malcolm and the Traitor.

[After routing a second usurper, Malcolm (Canmore) is crowned with great solemnity at Scone, and receives the oath of fealty from all who owe homage to the crown.]

In the crystyndome I trow than
Wes noucht in deid a bettyr man,
Na lyvand a bettyr knycht
Na mare manly, stowt, and wycht[1].
Amang all othir famows dedis
Mony men thus off hym redis[2];
That in hys court thare wes a knycht,
A lord off powere and off mycht,
That set hym till hawe slayne the kyng,
Hys purpos gyve he till end mycht bryng.
In-to the kyngys court than
Thare wes duelland a lele man
That tald the kyngys awyne persowne
That that lord set hym be tresowne
To sla the kyng, gyve that he
Mycht wyt[3] hys oportunyté.
This lord that tyme wes noucht present
In-to the court, bot wes absent,
Bot swne agayne he come wyth ma[4]
Than he wes wont, the kyng to sla.
Wyth curtasy yhit nevyretheles
Than, as befor, ressayvyd he wes.
The kyng than warnyd hys menyhé[5]
Wyth hym at hwntyng for to be;
And to that knycht he sayd alsua
That wyth hym-selff he wald hym ta[6]

[1] capable.

[2] recount.

[3] perceive.

[4] more.

[5] following.

[6] take.

By hym to syt at that huntyng.
The knycht consentyd to the kyng.
Than on the morne, wytht-owtyn let[1],
The setys and the stable sete[2],
The kyng and that lord alsua
Togydder rad, and nane bot tha,
Fere in the wode; and thare thay fand
A fayre brade land and a plesand,
A lytill hill off nobill ayre,
All wode abowt bathe thyk and fayre.

Than thus the kyng sayd to the knycht,
"On fwte at lykyng thow may lycht,
Or on hors gyve thow will be,
As the thynk best. Now ches thow the[3],
Horsyd and armyd als welle
As I am thow art ilke-dele[4].
Thi wapnys ar scharpe and mare redy
Than ony in-to this sted hawe I—
Dergat[5], spere, knyff, and swerd.
Betwene ws dele we now the werd[6].
Here is best now to begyn
Thi purpos, gyve thow will honowre wyn.
Here is nane that may ws se
Na help may owthir me or the,
For-thi [fande][7] now wyth all thi mycht
To do thi purpos as a knycht.
Set thow hawe fadyt thi lawté[8]
Do this dede yhit wyth honesté.
Gyve othir thow may or dare or wille,
Fenyhé the nowcht[9] to fulfille

[1] without hindrance.
[2] The points and positions being set.
[3] choose thou.
[4] every whit.
[5] Target.
[6] fate.
[7] Therefore try.
[8] Though thou hast failed in loyalty.
[9] Hesitate not.

Thi heycht[1], thi purpos, and thine athe.   [1] promise.
Do fourth thi dedys and be noucht lathe.
Gyve thow thynkys to sla me
Quhat tyme na nowe may bettyr be
Wytht fredome, or wyth mare manhed?
Or gyve thow wald put me to dede
Wyth venowme or wytht scharpe poysowne,
That is a wyffis condytyown.
Or gyve thow wald in-to my bede
Prevaly put me to dede,
That war as in adultery
Murthrysyd to be wnhonestly.
Or a knyff gyve thow wald hyd
Prewely, and thi tyme abyd
Quhill thow mycht at ese me sla,
A murtherere mycht do na war than sua[2].   [2] worse than so.
For-thi do as suld a knycht;
Ga we togyddyr, God dele the rycht!
Wyth oure foure handys and no ma;
Thare-on mot all the gamyn ga[3]."   [3] must all the game go.

    Wyth this the knycht all changyd hewe
Lyk hys purpos all to rewe,
And hys wysage worthyd wan[4]   [4] became pale.
As he had bene rycht a mad man.
Thare fell he downe and askyd mercy,
For all hys purpos wes foly,
And sayd his lord mycht wyth the lawe
Hym, as he was wald, bath hang and drawe;
And swa he yhald hym till hys will
On hym hys lust all to fulfill
Bwt ony kyn[5] condytyowne.   [5] Without any sort of.

The kyng than all his actyowne
Forgawe thi knycht thare qwytly,
And tuk hym all till his mercy;
And thare he become his man
Mare lele than he wes befor than.
And the kyng that wes hys lord
Let na man wyt off thare discord,

Till.   Quhill[1] the knycht hym-selff this cas
Tald in all as hapnyd was.

A Wedding Guest's Tale.

[Edward the Confessor dying childless in England, the throne
there is seized first by Harold, then by William of Normandy.
Upon this, Edgar Atheling, the lawful heir, being too young for
resistance, flies with his sisters Margaret and Christian. Their
ship is driven into the Firth of Forth, and they land at St.
Margaret's Hope. Christian takes the veil, but Margaret is
married by King Malcolm, and on the death of her brother
carries to the Scottish royal house the rightful succession to the
Saxon throne of England. Twice Malcolm raids the southern
kingdom, and once Scotland is wasted by William as far as
Abernethy. While invading England for the third time,
Malcolm and one of his sons are slain at Alnwick. The
crown, upon this, is seized by Malcolm's brother, Donald.
Donald is expelled by Duncan II., a natural son of Malcolm,
but two years later is reinstated by the Earl of Mearns.
Finally, after a reign of three years in all, Donald is over-
thrown, mutilated, and his eyes put out, and the kingdom is
held in turn by Malcolm's three sons, Edgar, Alexander I., and
David I. Edgar weds his sister Maud to Henry I. of England,
youngest son of the Conqueror. At the marriage there are
great rejoicings.]

2 feast.   Thare made wes a gret mawngery[2],

Quhare gaddryd ware the mast worthy,

3 degree.   And lordys off the grettast gre[3]

4 known.   That kend[4] ware in that cuntré.

Swa thare wes ane awlde knycht sete
Amang thame that day at the mete,
And thir wordys than said he:
" Now in the rwte is set the tre
Bathe frwyt and floure all lyk to bere."
Bot fewe wyst thare-off the manere.
Than thai reqwyryd hym that wes by
Sittand, to say per cumpany
Quhat sygnyfyid that mystyk word
That he swa spak than at the borde.
The knycht than sayd thame curtasly
He wald declere it oppynly.

" Quhille," he sayd, " I wes steward
Till my lord the King Edward,
And I before hym wes standand
At his mete, and he sittand
As he oysyd[1] wyth gret honowre,   1 used.
Thare wes a suspect traytoure,
Set[2] swa he wes nowcht prowyd in dede,   2 Though.
Yhit swilk he provyd or thine he yhed[3].   3 such he proved
                                                      ere thence he
By the kyng than at the mete   went.
He wes at his tabill sete.
In his hand a pes off brede
He had, that rycht thare made his dede.
For to the kyng this wes hys word
That day sittand at the bord,
' My lord, offt yhe have herd off me
That yhe suld betresyd be,
And that I suld be tresowne
Sla and wndo yhoure persowne.

Gyve evyr I thowcht for to do sua

I pra God hyne¹ I neẅyre ga,

Bot at this ilk² pes of bred

Here at yhoure bord be now my dede,

And off it nevyr a crote,

Quhill I be wyrryd³, owre-pas my throt.'

That brede than he begouth till ete,

Bot owre hys throt it mycht noucht get.

Swa, suddanly rycht at the borde

He wyrryd, and spak neẅyre a word

Mare than he spak of that bred

Before that he deyd in that stede.

The kyng than gert hym doggydly

Be drawyn owt, and dyspytwsly⁴

Oure a hewch⁵ gert cast hym downe,

Doggys till ete his caryowne.

My lord," he sayd, yhit sittand

As in a study [than] musand,

And efftyr that all this was done

As yhe have herd, than sayd he sone,

As vaknyd⁶ owt off his study.

"I wes," he sayd, "in Normandy

Bydand⁷, as yhe wyst, a quhille

Owt off this land in gret exyle;

And swa thare wes twa cunnand men

That offt to me repayryd then,

My specyall famylyerys,

Off plesand and off fayre manerys.

The state off Ingland on a day

Be thare word sare menyd⁸ thai,

¹ hence.
² that this same.
³ Till I be choked.
⁴ without pity.
⁵ crag.
⁶ wakened.
⁷ Abiding.
⁸ lamented.

And sayd Ingland wes lyk to be
Confowndyd for gret inyqwyté
That wes done in-to that land;
For few in it wes than lyvand
That wes commendyd all ẅertuws,
Bot iẅill and fals and lycherus,
[And] nowthir lauch na [yhit] lawté[1]   [1] law nor loyalty.
Wes oysyd na done in that cuntré,
And lordys be thare aẅarys
The sympill folk wald ay supprys;
Byschapys, prestys, and prelatys
In hawtayne[2] pryd ay led thare statys;   [2] haughty.
Swa, lyk war[3], that inyqwyté   [3] likely it was.
Suld all wndo this hale[4] cuntré.   [4] whole.
I askyd," he sayd, "than, qwhat remede
This mycht helpe or stand in sted.
Ane off thame than awnsweryd me
And sayd, 'Swilk[5] help may fall to be,   [5] Such.
As be this ryddill I will the say,
Fra the or [I sall] pas away.
A grene tre fra the rwte wes sawyn,
And fra it a space wes drawyn,
As men for till wndyrstand,
Large thre akyre leynth off land.
This tre may happyn for to get
The kynd rwte, and in it be set,
And sap to recovyr syne
Bath [the] leyff and flewowre fyne,
And the froyte the tre oure-sprede.
Than is to lyppyn[6] sum remede.'"   [6] to be expected.

Than the knycht sayd, "Now I se
In-to the kynd rwte set the tre.
This tre yhe may wndyrstand
To be the kynryk off Ingland
That in honowre and ryches
And in gret welth abowndand wes.
The rwte, yhe trow, kyngys sede
Quhare-off all kyngis come on dede,
That awcht[1] the kynryk off Ingland,
Be lyne and lynage discendand,
Quhill[2] Harald, Bastard, and Willame Rede,
That now in mwld ar lyand dede,
Off that state interruptyowne.
Mad be thare intrusyowne.
Thir ware the akyr-leynthis thre
That before rehersyd we;
Ilkane off thir[3] wyth thare streynth
Fychyd[4] the tre ane akyr-leynth.
Now gottyn has that tre the rwte
Off kynd[5], oure confort and oure bute[6],
All lyk to bere bath frwyt and floure
In-till oure helpe and oure succoure,
Syne[7] Saxon and the Scottys blude
Togyddyr is in yhon frely fwde[8],
Dame Mald, our qwene and oure lady,
Now weddyd wyth oure kyng Henry."

This knycht syttand at the borde
All this rehers[it] word be word.

[1] owned.

[2] Till.

[3] Each one of these.
[4] Fetched.

[5] nature (the native root).
[6] good.

[7] Since.

[8] noble person.

The Burial of Henry II. of England.

[David I. founds no fewer than five bishoprics and nine or ten abbeys, and marries the heiress of the Earl of Huntingdon, through whom that earldom is inherited by the Scottish kings. He makes war upon the usurper Stephen in support of the claims of his niece Maud to the English throne, but is defeated in a great battle (Battle of the Standard). The crown of England, however, is settled on Maud's son, afterwards Henry II., and David obtains Northumberland and Cumberland. In this reign the deposed Donald, though blind and emasculate, accomplishes a terrible revenge. Desponding one day on his hard fate, he hears the king's son, "a gangand bairn," go by. He calls to the child, who comes innocently to be kissed, when Donald so handles him that he screams and dies. At this sight the queen, too, suddenly expires, and the succession itself is only saved by the Cæsarean operation. Donald is cast into a dungeon and starved to death. David's remaining son, Prince Henry, Earl of Huntingdon and Northumberland, dying, to the great grief of the kingdom, before his father, that king is succeeded in turn by his grandsons, Malcolm the Maiden and William the Lion. In the reign of the latter monarch Scotland loses all her recent acquisitions. Surprised and captured at Alnwick, William is only freed on condition of relinquishing important possessions and paying homage to Henry. These exactions are considered the greater hardship since William's grandfather David himself knighted Henry at Carlisle, and passing to London, set him on the English throne. Scotland, nevertheless, suffers great depression till the death of the English king. His burial is described.]

Quhen this Henry thus wes dede,
For to be borne to the sted
Ordanyd for hys sepulture,
As suld a dede kyng wyth honwre,
Hys body oure wes cled all hale
In honest kyngys aparale;
Till hys fete fra hys heẅyd[1] all downe,   [1] head.
Haẅand thare-on off gold a crowne,
And gluẅys on his handys twa,
Beltyd wyth his suerd alsua,

Septyr, [and] ryng, and sandallys

Browdyn[1] welle on kyngys wys,
Bot hys visage wes all bare.
Thus bore wyth lordys that ware thare
To the sted off hys sepulture
Wyth gret reverens and honwre.
Rychard hys swn than and his ayre
Wyth hys court plesand and rycht fayre
Than mete hys fadyr on the way.
Off that dede body, quhare it lay,
Owt off the nesthryllys twa
The red blud brystyd owt, that sua
Fast it bled that all thare-by

Gangand had thare-off ferly[2].

How ilkane kest[3] in thaire intent
Thare wes na certane jwgement,
Bot lyk it wes be that thyng sene

That the spyryt wes movyd in tene[4]
Off the fadyre agayne the swne.
Yhit nevyrtheles, all to be dwne,

This Rychard passyd on, gretand sare[5],
Wyth lordys that the body bare
To the sted off the sepulture,
Quhare it interyd wes wyth honwre.

Efftyre tha exeqwyis als fast

Till Lwndyn this ilk[6] Rychard past,
And tuk thi crowne in-to the sted
Off hys fadyr that thus wes dede.
Set he Rychard be name wes cald,
For he a stowt knycht and a bald

Wes in prys[1] off hys renowne.   [1] praise.
Rychard the hart off a lyowne,
Or Lyownys Hart to say schortly,
Thai cald this Rychard comownaly.
Till oure kyng Willame he qwhylum wes[2]   [2] sometime was.
Luẅyd falow in dedys off prowes ;
For-thi thai war ilkane till othir
Specyalle, as he had bene his brodyr.

[With a sum of ten thousand marks (£100,000 sterling) William recovers from Richard all his dignities, estates, and homages, and he renders important assistance to the English king both in setting out for and in returning from his Crusade. For a few chapters further the events of the two countries are narrated together. On the southern side are related the quarrels of King John with church and barons, and the consequent invasion of England and capture of London by Louis, the Dauphin of France. In the north, for his share in these troubles, Alexander II., William the Lion's son, suffers excommunication, and among other matters an account is given of a clan feud between the Besats of Oban and the men of Athole. In 1242 the king and queen with their court are entertained for a night by Sir William Besat at Oban. Next morning the king hastens away to Edinburgh, leaving the queen behind. Four days later she rides to Forfar, attended by Sir William. That night, after attending a tournament at Haddington, Patrick, Earl of Athole, and his company are burnt "to coals" in their lodging. For this deed Besat and his two brothers are blamed. In vain it is shown that on the fatal night Sir William sat late at supper with the queen in Forfar, and led her to her chamber before retiring himself. In vain the queen offers to swear in person to his innocence. In vain Besat himself has the misdoers cursed "wyth buk and bell" in all the kirks of the diocese of Aberdeen, and offers to prove his innocence upon the bodies of his accusers. It is asserted that, wherever he himself might be that night, his arms and men were seen in Haddington, and that the deed was done by the Besats for an ancient feud. Their lands are harried utterly of goods and cattle, and before the fury of the powerful kinsmen of Athole, they are finally banished the kingdom.]

Lament for Alexander III.

[On the death of Alexander II. in 1249, his son Alexander III.,
eight years of age, is crowned at Scone. A year later he is
married to Margaret, daughter of Henry III. of England.
Henry intrigues to the prejudice of Scotland, and, at home,
struggles occur between the barons of English and Scottish
interest for possession of the king. In 1263, however, Alex-
ander has asserted himself, and fights the battle of Largs, where,
amid a tempest of "gret weddrys scharpe and snell," the Norse
ascendancy over the Western Isles is finally broken. Among
further particulars detailed of the time of Alexander III. the
right of coining money is confirmed to the Church; Edward I.
conquers Wales; and in Dunfermline at the translation of St.
Margaret, a miracle happens, her body refusing to be lifted till
that of her husband Malcolm has first been removed. Upon
the king's death his wise government receives justice at the
hands of the poet.]

A thowsand twa hundyr foure score off yhere
The fyft, fra that the Madyn clere
Jhesu Cryst oure Lord had borne,
Alysandyr oure kyng deyd at Kyngorne.
Fra that place he wes had syne[1]
And enteryd in Dwnfermlyne.
In that collegyd kyrk he lyis
Hys spyryt in-till paradys.

Scotland menyd hym than full sare[2],
For wndyr hym all his legis ware
In honoure, qwyete, and in pes,
For-thi cald PESSYBILL KYNG he wes.
He honoryd God and Haly Kyrk,
And medfull dedys he oysyd to wyrk.
Till all prestys he dyd reverens,
And sawffyd[3] thare statys wyth diligens.
He [was] stedfast in crystyn fay;

[1] afterwards.
[2] lamented him sore.
[3] preserved.

Relygyows men he honoryde ay.
He luẅyd all men that [war] ẅertuows;
He lathyd and chastyd [all] vytyows.
Be justys he gave and eqwyté
Till ilke man that his suld be.
That he mycht noucht till ẅertu drawe
He held ay wndyr dowt[1] and awe.

  [1] fear.

He gert chasty[2] mysdoarys
As lauch wald be thare manerys.

  [2] caused chastise.

The lawch he gert be kepyd welle
In all his kynryk ilka delle.
He led his lyff in honesté,
Devotyown, and chastyté.
Till lordys, knychtys, and sqwyerys
That ware plesand off manerys
He wes lele, luẅand, and liberale,
And all ẅertuows in governale.
He wes gret off almows dede[3]
Till all that he couth wyt had nede.

  [3] deeds of alms.

Yhwmen, powere karl, or knaẅe,
That wes off mycht an ox til haẅe
He gert that man haẅe part in pluche[4].

  [4] ploughing.

Swa wes corne in [his] land enwche.
Swa than begowth[5], and efftyr lang
Off land wes mesure, ane ox-gang.

  [5] began.

Mychty men, that had ma
Oxyn, he gert in pluchys ga.
A pluch of land efftyr that
To nowmyr[6] off oxyn mesuryd gat.

  [6] number.

Be that vertu all hys land
Off corn he gert be abowndand.

A bolle off atys[1] pennys foure

Off Scottys moné past noucht oure[2];
A boll off bere for awcht or ten
In comowne prys sawld wes then;
For sextene a boll of qwhete,
Or for twenty, the derth wes grete.
This falyhyd fra he deyd suddanly;

This sang wes made off hym for-thi[3].

[CANTUS.]

Quhen Alysandyr owre Kyng wes dede,

That Scotland led in luẅe and le[4],

Away wes sons[5] off ale and brede,
Off wyne and wax, off gamyn and gle.
Oure gold wes changyd in-to lede.—
Cryst, borne in-to Vyrgynyté,
Succoure Scotland and remede,
That stad [is in] perplexyté.

The Lady Devorgil.

[David and Alexander, the sons of Alexander III., having died childless before their father, and his daughter, married to Eric of Norway, having left only the young Margaret, "the Maid of Norway," Edward I. asks this princess in marriage for his son. She dies, however, before reaching Scotland. The case of the Scottish succession is then stated at great length, John Balliol claiming the throne as grandson of the eldest daughter, and Robert Bruce as son of the youngest daughter of David, brother of William the Lion. The lineal descent of the Comyns is also traced from the dethroned King Donald. A legend like that of the Lady Godiva is related of Maud, queen of Henry I., and a quaint story is told of the mother of Balliol.]

Now to rehers it is my will
Sum ẅertws dedis off Derẅorgill.
That lady wcs, as I herd say,
Alanys [douchtyr] off Gallway.
Jhon eldare Ballyoll in his lyffe
That lady weddyt till his wyff,
And on hyr syne efftyr that
Jhon the Ballyoll the kyng he gat.
Quhen the Ballyoll [at]¹ wes hyr lord   ¹ that.
Spowsyd, as yhe herd record,
Hys sawle send till his Creature,
Or he wes layd in sepulture
Scho gert oppyn his body tyte²,   ² quickly.
And gert his hart be tane owt qwyte³.   ³ had his heart
Wyth spycery welle savorand,   taken out
And off kynd welle flevorand,   whole.
That ilke hart than, as men sayd,
Scho bawmyd, and gert it be layd
In-till a cophyn off evore⁴   ⁴ ivory.
That scho gert be made tharefore,
Annamalyd and perfytly dycht⁵,   ⁵ Enamelled and
Lokyt, and bwndyn wyth sylver brycht.   perfectly
And alway quhen scho yhed till mete⁶   polished.
That [cophyne scho gert by hir] sett, ⁶ went to meat.
And till hyr lord, as in presens,
Ay to that scho dyd reverens.
And thare scho gert set ilka day,
[As] wont before hyr lord wes ay,
All the cowrssys coẅeryd welle
In-to sylver brycht ẅeschelle
Browcht fra the kychyn and thare set.

Quhen scho mad hyr to rys fra met
All thai courssys scho gert then
Be tane wp and delt til pure men;
Scho send all thai courssys gud,

¹ chose.
As scho thame chesyt¹, to ta thare fude.
This scho cessyt nevyr to do
Quhill lyvand in this warld wes scho.
Scho ordanyt in hyre testament
And gave byddyng wyth hale intent
That that hart thai suld than ta
And lay it betwene hyr pappys twa,

² bound in duty.
As detyt² thai war than wyth honowre
To lay hyr wyth that in sepulture.

Scho fowndyt in-to Gallway
Off Cystews ordyre ane abbay.
Dulce-Cor scho gert thaim all,
That is Swet-Hart, that abbay call;
And now the men off Gallway
Callys that sted the New Abbay.
Howssys off freris scho fwndyt tway;
Wygtowne and Dunde [war] thai.

³ enlargement.
In ekyng³ als off Goddis serẅyce
Scho fowndyt in Glasgow twa chapellanyis,
And in the Universyté
Off Oxynfurde scho gert be
A collage fowndyt.* This lady
Dyd all thir dedis devotly.

* Balliol College.

A bettyr lady than scho wes nane
In all the yle off Mare Bretane.
Scho wes rycht plesand off bewté;
Here wes gret taknys off bownté[1].   [1] token of worth.

The Sack of Berwick.

[Balliol accepts the crown as a vassal of Edward, but presently,
resisting the indignities put upon him, is deprived of his honours
by the English king. In support of the falling monarch three
hundred gentlemen of Fife attack Berwick and carry it at the
point of the sword.]

Quhen the Kyng Edward off Ingland
Had herd off this deid full tythand[2]   [2] tidings.
All breme he belyd in-to berth[3],   [3] furious he blazed into wrath.
And wrythyd all in wedand werth[4],   [4] in raging state.
Alsa kobbyd in his crope[5]   [5] choked in his gullet.
As he had ettyn ane attyrcope[6];   [6] eaten a spider.
And als fast assemblyd hys ost,
And come to Berwyk wyth gret bost,
And layd a sege to the town,
Assawtis makand rycht fellown[7].   [7] Making right fierce assaults.
The stwff[8] wythin resystens   [8] garrison.
Agayne hym made, and gret deffens.
Sa qwhene he saw that he mycht noucht
The town off were[9] wyn as he thoucht,   [9] by war.
Wndyr dissymbelatyown
Bath tent thai tuk wp and pawillown,
All lyk as to gere cese that were;
Than he removyd wyth his powere,

And scalyd in buschementis¹ nere thareby
His ostys, bydand prewally

² Letting pass.
Owrdrywand² a day or twa.
And qwhill that thai war bydand swa
Thai fenyhyd armys off Scotland

³ knew.
As thai kend³ lordis thai berand;
And ayrly on the Gud Fryday
To the town agayne come thai,
The lordis armys off Scotland
At the sown ryssyng apperand
On bayneris payntyd and penownys.

Wythin the town the Scottis wes
Rejosyd in-till gret blythnes
Off that sycht; for thai wyst noucht
Off the desayt agayne thame wroucht,
Bot thai trowyd that thaire kyng
That ost hade sende in thare helpyng.

⁴ gates.
For-thi the yhettis⁴ alsa fast
All off the towne thai gert wp cast.
And at thai yhettis oppyn then
Fast thrang [in] the Inglys men,
And wmbeset the Scottis thare
Or thai wyst welle quhat thai ware.
The Inglis [men] thare slwe downe
[All] hale the Scottis natyowne
That wyth-in that towne thai fand,
Off all condytyowne nane sparand;

⁵ Cleric and lay
Leryd and lawde⁵, nwne and frere,
All wes slayne wyth that powere;

Off allkyn state, off allkyn age,
[Thai] sparyd nothir carl na page;
Bath awld and yhowng, men and wyẅys,
And sowkand barnys thar tynt[1] thare lyvys;   [1] unweaned
                                                infants there
Yhwmen and gentilmen alsa,   lost.
The lyvys all thai tuk [thaim] fra.
Thare slayne wes downe the floure of Fyffe;
Thare sawlys to sawff thai spendyt the lyffe,
And in the sawfté off the town
Before, thai had the mast renown.

Thus thai slayand ware sa fast
All the day, qwhill[2] at the last   [2] till.
This Kyng Edward saw in that tyde
A woman slayne, and off hyr syde
A barne he saw fall owt, sprewland
Besyd that woman slayne lyand.
"*Lasses, Lasses*," than cryid he;
"Leve off, leve off," that word suld be.

Sevyn thowsand and fyve hundyr ware
Bodyis reknyd that slayne ware thare.
This dwne wes on the Gud Fryday.
Off elde na kynd nane sparyd thai.
Twa dayis owt, as a depe flwde,
Throw all the town thare ran rede blude.
Thus that Kyng of Ingland,
Noucht kyng, bot a fell tyrand,
Led that day his devotyown.

He gert thare thole the passyown

Off dede¹ mony a creature

In-till gratyous state and pure,

Clene schrewyn, in gud entent

Redy to tak thare sacrament.

Hys offyce wes that Gud Fryday

Till here innocentis de, and say

"Allace! allace! now, Lord, we cry,

For hym that deyd that day, mercy!"

Nane othir serwys that day herd he,

Bot gert thame slay on, but peté.²

The sawlys that he gert slay down thare

He send quhare his sawle nevyrmare

Wes lyk to come, that is the blys,

Quhare alkyn joy ay lestand is.

A Border Tournament.*

[The rise of Sir William Wallace, his victory over the English
Treasurer at Stirling Bridge, and his defeat at Falkirk, follow.
Edward subdues all south of the Forth, and harries his opponents
as far as Perth, "noucht levand behynd bot wattyr and stane.
The three great battles at Roslyn are described, in which in one
day twenty thousand English are defeated by Sir John Comyn
and Sir Simon Fraser; and Edward's capture of Stirling is
narrated. But for the rest of the Wars of Succession the reader
of the *Cronykil* is referred to Barbour. On the death of Bruce
the regency of Randolph and his shrewd administration of justice
are detailed, his policy being to make the sheriff personally
responsible for gear stolen in each district. The regent, however,
is poisoned at a feast at Wemyss; whereupon Edward Balliol
lands at Kinghorn, wins the great battle of Dupplin near Perth,
and is crowned at Scone. The wars of the Wardens of Scotland

---

* The description of this tournament forms part of the MS.
interpolated in his narrative by Wyntoun.

against Balliol and Edward III. ensue at great length, the most outstanding episodes of the narrative being the hanging of Sir Alexander Seton's son before the eyes of his father and mother because Seton will not deliver Berwick to the English king earlier than the time agreed, the slaughter of 10,000 Scots at the great battle of Halidon Hill, and the spirited and success-ful defence of Dunbar by its countess. In this defence it is narrated how, when a boulder from one of Montague's catapults would strike the ramparts,

> Wyth a towalle a damyselle
> Arayid jolyly and welle
> Wipyt the walle, that thai mycht se,
> To gere thaim mare anoyid be.

In particular, an illustration of the chivalry of that day is afforded by a description of a great jousting at Berwick in 1338.]

Off Lancastyr Schyr Henry,
That callyd than wes Erle of Derby,
Than wyth the kyng wes rycht prewe.
On Scotlandis marchis trawelyd he
And had gret yharnyng to wyn prys[1].
He wes ay worthy, wycht, and wys,
And mast renownyd off bownté,
Off gentrys[2], and off honesté,
That in-till Ingland lywand was.
He has herd spek how the Dowglas
Throw wyt and wyrschipe apertly[3]
Dyd mony dowchty jwperty[4].
He send and askyd thre cours off were
At hym, and he grawntyt it there.
Thai come samyn[5] at a certane plas.
Alysawndyre the Ramsay thare was
Serwand Dowglas at that justyng,
For he expart wes in-tyll swilk thyng[6].
The nobill Erle off Derby
Come wyth a joly cumpany.

[1] yearning to earn praise.

[2] gentlehood.

[3] boldly.

[4] many doughty enterprises.

[5] together.

[6] such things.

Sone fra thai hade thair salus made,
Thai tuk thare rynkis, and samyn rade.
And at the tothir[1] cours off were
The Dowglas hit and brak his spere,
And a sclys off the schafft that brak
In-till his hand a wounde can mak.
Tharefore the gud Erle off Derby,
That saw hym hurt sa fellownly[2],
Wald thole[3] hym than to just no mare.
Bot, or[4] he tuk his leve to fare,
He spak till Alysawndyr Ramsay,
And specyally kan[5] hym pray
For to purchas a cumpany,
That at the lest thai war twenty,
Off gentill-men wyth scheld and spere,
To just ilk man thre cowrs off were;
And gyve he na had all gentillmen,
He bad tak knawyn yhwmen then,
To cum to Berwyk a set day.
Thare-till grawntyd the Ramsay,
And sayd that he suld welle purchas
Cumpany, and cum to that plas,
Wytht thi[6] [that] thai all assuryd ware,
Quhat-evyr than fell at that justyng thare.

The Erle thame assuryd willfully,
Ande the Ramsay in well gret hy
Gat hym falowys, and at the day
To Berwyk come, bathe he and thai.
The Erle ressayẅyd thame curtasly,
And gert delyẅere thame herbry[7].

Apon the morne, qwhen that thai ware
Makand thame bowne[1], hym-selff come thare,   [1] ready.
And fand all oppyn the entré,
And noucht-for-thi[2] thare knokide he   [2] notwithstanding.
Wyth-owte the dure all prewally,
Quhill Ramsay til hym [coym] in hy
[And] gert hym entre sone. Than he
Sayd, " God mot at yhoure laykyng be![3]"   [3] God help your desire.
Syne said he, " Lordis, on qwhat manere
Will yhe ryn at this justyng here?"
" Wyth plate scheldis," sayd Ramsay,
" As it afferis[4] to this play."   [4] is proper.
" A! syrrys, be oure Lord," sayd he,
" So suld no man here prysyt be[5],   [5] be praised.
For none till othir mycht do iwill.
Bot and it likand[6] ware yhow till   [6] agreeable.
As men hostayis for to ryn[7]   [7] to run in fashion of war.
So mycht men prys off wyrschype wyne."
Quod Alysawndyre the Ramsay,
" It sall lik til ws all, perfay,
That ilk man ryn his falow till
In kyrtill allane, gyve that yhe will."
The Erle sayd than debonarly,
" Nay, that is all to hard trewly."
Quod Willame off the Towris than,
" Schyre, gyve yhe na will, lat ilke man
Ryn all bare wysage, and yhe
Qwha [eschewis] fyrst rycht swne sall se."
The Erle sayde mekilly, " Schyris, nay,
Yhit that is all to hard, perfay[8];   [8] i' faith.
Bot as I said yhowe will ye do,

Than suld sum prys folow ws to."
Thaire-to thai gave all thare consent,
And he furth till his falowys went.

The justyng lestyd dayis thre,

Qwhare men apert[1] cowrsis mycht se.
Twa Inglis knychtis thare ware slayne;
Off Scottis men there deyde nane;
Bot turnand hamwart be the way
Off ane hurt endyt Jhone the Hay;
And Willame the Ramsay wes there
Borne throw the heẅyd wyth a spere,
And throw the helme wyth strynth off hand,

2 Till the shaft
  stayed sticking
  there.
Qwhill the trwnsowne [bad] thare stekand[2].
3 quickly.
Thai browcht a preste till hym belyẅe[3],
And in his helme he can hym schryẅe.
Than sayd the gud Erle of Derby,

4 surely.
" Lo! heyre a fayre sycht sykkyrly[4].
A fayrere sycht how ma man se
Than knycht or sqwyere, quhethir-evyr he be,

5 in this fashion.
In-till his helme hym thus-gat[5] schryẅe?
Qwhen I sall pas owt off this lyve
I wald God off his grace wald send
To me on swylk manere till end."
Qwhen he had schryẅyn hym, as I say,
Alysawndyr than the Ramsay

6 without delay.
Gert lay hym down forowtyn lete[6],
And on his helme his fute he sete,

7 wrench.
And wyth gret strynth owt can aras[7]
The trownsown that thare stekand was.
He rase allane fra it wes owte,

And wyth a gud will and a stowte
He sayd that he wald [ayl] na-thyng.
Tharoff the Eile had wonderyng,
And gretly hym commendit then,
And sayd, " Lw ! stowt hartis off men."

Thus hapnyd till hym off this lame[1].
And a gud knycht, Patrik the Grame,
That had traẅellyd beyhond the se
Till eyk his prys[2] throw gret bownté,
He herd spek off this justyng gretly,
And sped hym thiddyr in all hy.
He come thiddyr on the tothir day[3];
Than Rýchard Talbot can hym pray
To serẅe hym off thre cours off were,
And he thaim grawntyt but dawngere.
Sone efftyr samyn can thai ryne[4].
The Talbot on had platis twyne[5],
And throw thame bath his spere he bare,
And in the brest ane inch or mare.
Had he jwstyd as conand was[6]
He had bene dede in-to that plas.
Thare coursis haly can thai ma,
Bot nane had mare harme off thai twa.

The Talbot syne can hym requere
To be wyth hym at the supere.
He assentyt, and qwhen thai were
Syttand best at the supere
Thar salute thaim a cumly knycht,

[1] on this ground.

[2] To add to his praise.

[3] second day.

[4] began to run together.
[5] twain.

[6] as was agreed.

That semyt stowt, bath bald and wycht,
And amang thare gud wordis there
At Schyr Patryk three courss off were
He askyd in-to gud cumpany;
And he, as burdand, sayd smethely[1]
"Man, will thow have off me justyng?
Rys up to-morn in the mornyng,
And here thi mes[2] welle, and schrywe the;
And thow sall sone delyveryt be."
He made tharoff na gabbyng[3],
For on the morn at the justyng
He bare hym throw the body qwhit
And he deyt off the dynt welle tyte[4].

This was upon the thryde day,
And quhen justyt ilkane had thai
The haraldis sayd than on this wys,
That gud ware to gyff the prys,
On athyre halff to mak thaim mede,
That bare thame best, for thare gud dede.
The lordis gawe assent thare-till,
And ordanyt wyth thaire allaris will[5]
That Inglis suld the Scottis prys[6],
And thai thaim on the samyn wys.

The Inglis men the prys gaffe than
Till ane that thre halle[7] courssis ran
And forowtyn hyt[8]. Bot Scottis men
Awysit thaim alsamyn then[9],
And till the knycht the prys gawe thai
That smate Wilyame the Ramsay

Throw-owte the hede; and a skyll[1]
Thai schawyt till enfors thare-till[2],
And sayd it wes justyng off were,
And [he] that mast engrewyt[3] there
Suld have the gretast prys, wyth thi[4]
That he engrewyt honestly.
The haraldis than can say haly
The dome wes suthfast and worthy[5];
Tharfor sayd ane, "Me-thynk, perfay,
That he that a knycht yhistyrday
Slwe, and ane othir to-day, the prys
Suld have, Patrik the Grame that is.
For hade the Talbot as taylyd was[6]
Justyd, he had swelt[7] in-to that plas.
As to this prys-gywyng, for-thi,
I hald hym dede all wtraly."
On this wys spak the haraldis thare,
Bot, for the prys wes gywyn are[8],
Thai wald repelle it be na way.

And than the gud Erle can say,
" I trow it has bene seldyn sene
That off were justyng thus has bene
Contenyt[9] thre dayis, and the prys
Gywyn as at this jwstyng is."
He festaid the jwstarys that day,
That on the morne syne held thaire way.

[1] reason.
[2] showed to clinch (their decision).
[3] did most vex-ing.
[4] with this (con-dition).
[5] true and gallant.
[6] as was cove-nanted.
[7] died.
[8] before.
[9] Conducted.

[By the efforts of Douglas, Ramsay, and the Warden, Robert Stewart, the English ascendency is gradually overcome, and David II. is brought home from France, whither he had been sent. Presently, however, at the request of the French king, he invades England, and with several of his nobles is taken prisoner

at the battle of Durham.   In 1349 the "first pestilence"
destroys a third of the population of Scotland.   On the death of
David II. the crown passes to the Stewarts in the person of
Robert II.   The growth of friendly relations with France is
narrated, the bond of union being the common hostility to
England.   In a long narrative of Border warfare the most
conspicuous event is the defeat and capture of Percy at Otter-
bourne.   Several tournaments in France and England are
described, as well as the fight between Clan Chattan and Clan
Quhele ("the thretty for thretty") in barriers before the king at
Perth.   Then follow the dethronement of Richard of England
by Henry IV., and the cruel death at Falkland of the son of
Robert III., David, Duke of Rothesay,

> Cunnand in-to litterature
> A seymly persone in stature.

At Homildon in 1402, Murdoch Stewart and the Earl of
Douglas are defeated by Percy with great loss.   Douglas, taken
prisoner, is made to join Percy in the battle against Henry IV.
at Shrewsbury.   The circumstances are detailed of the seizure
at sea by the English of Robert's remaining son, Prince James.
Robert III. dies at Dundonald, and during the ensuing regency
of the Duke of Albany the chronicle ends with the expedition
into Flanders of Scottish knights errant under the Earl of Mar.]

HENRY THE MINSTREL.

HENRY THE MINSTREL.

ALTHOUGH a new fashion had been set for the more polite poetry of Scotland by the example of King James I. in the early part of the fifteenth century, much of the popular verse of the country continued to flow in the older channels. Of this there exist several specimens. Besides popular ballads like *The Battle of Harlaw*,[1] which was probably composed soon after the event which it celebrates, in 1411, there remain such compositions as *The Howlat, or The Danger of Pride*,[2] a long moral fable in the obscure style of *Gawen and Gologras*, supposed to have been written about 1450 by Sir Richard Holland, a partizan of the house of Douglas; and a curious rugged performance in various measures, called *Cockelbie's Sow*,[3] conveying in a vein of quaint rustic humour a recommendation of such virtues as almsgiving and economy.

But by far the best and most important of all these compositions is the great popular epic of the people's

---

[1] Printed in Ramsay's "Evergreen."
[2] Pinkerton's "Ancient Scottish Poems."
[3] Laing's "Select Remains of the Ancient Popular Poetry of Scotland."

hero, *The Actis and Deidis of the Illustere and Vailyeand
Campioun, Schir William Wallace, Knicht of Ellerslie.*
Here, in flowing minstrel verse, not without fire and
a certain heroic ring, is preserved an example, perhaps
the last, of the bardic narratives which, chanted in
hall and hostelrie, stirred the blood and regaled the
time in Scotland in the long rush-lit evenings of the
fifteenth century.   And here, coloured somewhat
perhaps by the two hundred years of interval between
subject and singer, but not the less interesting on that
account, remains the great store of fact and legend
concerning the knight who, short as was his career
and cruel as was his fate, struck the blow which
wakened Scotland to life.

Of the author of the poem, Henry the Minstrel, or
"Blind Harry," as from his infirmity he used to be
popularly called, very little has been recorded.   John
Mair, who was born about 1454, mentions him in his
history.   "In the time of my infancy," he says,
"Henry, a man blind from his birth, composed the
whole *Book of William Wallace,* and committed to
writing in vernacular poetry, in which he was skilled,
the things which were commonly related.   I, however,
give only partial credit to such writings.   By the
recitation of these stories in the presence of men of
foremost rank he procured food and clothing, of which
he was worthy."   Of himself the poet says, "It is weill
knawin I am a bural (rustic) man;" and more than
once he deprecates criticism on account of his
situation.   Near the end of the last book he says :

All worthi men at redys this rurall dyt
Blaym nocht the buk, set I be wnperfyt.

I suld hawe thank sen I nocht trawaill spard ;
For my laubour na man hecht me reward ;
Na charge I had off king nor othir lord ;
Gret harm I thocht his gud deid suld be smord.
I haiff said her ner as the process gais,
And fenyeid nocht for frendschip nor for fais.
Costis herfor was no man bond to me ;
In this sentence I had na will to be.

Further, in the Treasury accounts of James IV. there
appear several entries of gratuities to Henry. The
last of these entries occurs in January, 1492, and it is
supposed, therefore, that he died before the end of
the century.

Nothing more is known of the poet's life. Of his
character it is only possible to read something between
the lines of his work. There a rough, uncom-
promising patriot is seen, honestly anxious to exalt the
national hero, and bitter as a man of limited
knowledge, circumscribed by his blindness and the
spirit of his time, was likely to be against his country's
enemies.

As with the *King's Quair*, a single manuscript has
transmitted the Minstrel's work to modern times.
It is bound up with the MS. of Barbour's *Bruce*,
written by the same scribe, John Ramsay, in 1488,
and preserved in the Advocates' Library. Set down
during the poet's lifetime, this copy is likely to be
fairly correct, though there are some ten or twelve
lines throughout the work which are hardly intel-
ligible. The Minstrel's inability to put his own
composition on paper would sufficiently account for
more than these. Of printed editions the earliest

known is that of 1570 by "Robert Lekprevik at the Expensis of Henrie Charteris," of which only one copy is known to exist (in the British Museum). There have been many later editions, but the best are one of Perth in 1790, Dr. Jamieson's in 1820, and one for the Scottish Text Society by Mr. James Moir in 1885.

The poem is divided into eleven books, and is written in the ten-syllable line rhyming in couplets, which had been wrought to great perfection by Chaucer, and has since been accorded the title of heroic verse.

Beyond an allusion or two to "Ector of Troy" and the like, which were probably the common stock of minstrels of his time, the poet does not display an acquaintance with the ancient classics. On the other hand he seems to have studied not only the style, but the sentiment and even the structure of the romances of chivalry which still at that period formed a large part of minstrel entertainment. Many of the expressions which he uses appear to be borrowed directly from these models. Phrases like "Wapynnys stiff of steill," and "In armys sone he coucht that queyn with croun," strike as a direct echo from poems like *Sir Tristrem.* The ellipses, too, which are his constant habit, find a parallel in such work as the Rhymer's. It need not be marvelled at, therefore, if the influence of these romance models made itself further felt, and if the Minstrel sought to run the half-legendary incidents of his hero's life themselves into the conventional mould. The historical credit due to Henry's *Wallace* has been debated by nearly every editor who has undertaken the reproduction of the poem, but by none does this romance influence appear to have been taken into sufficient consideration. Henry declares in his work that he got his materials from a Latin history of the hero written by John Blair, Wallace's own schoolfellow and chaplain; and from frequent references throughout the poem the existence of such a work seems beyond doubt. In the tenth book, after recording a fight with the pirate, John of Lynn, in which Blair acted a valiant part, the Minstrel adds:

> Bot maister Blayr spak nothing off himsell
> In deid off armes quhat awentur he fell;
> Schir Thomas Gray, was than preyst to Wallace,
> Put in the buk how than hapnyt this cace.

The character of Blair's history itself cannot now be judged. Sir Robert Sibbald, indeed, published a work, *Relationes Arnaldi Blair*; but this has been shown to be a mere series of extracts from the *Scotichronicon.* In any case, however, it is reasonable to believe that with the materials of Blair's history Henry inwove the legends of Wallace current in his own time. The knight of Ellerslie, to be a leader at all in those days, must have been a man of immense physical strength; but the superhuman feats occasionally attributed to him by the poet are beyond reasonable belief, and can only be accounted for by the understanding that they were owed to popular tradition, which in two hundred years had had time to magnify the hero's deeds. It is not probable and hardly possible that some of these stories—episodes in which whole troops are mowed down by the single arm of Wallace—could be derived as they stand from the sober contemporary record of an eye-witness like the chaplain.   Henry on his last page confesses regarding at least one episode :

> Thir twa gert me say that ane othir wyss ;
> Till Maister Blayr we did sumpart off dispyss.

The fact appears to be that in the Minstrel's time Wallace had already become a half-mythical figure round whose deeds the national imagination had gathered a literature of legend.   Wyntoun said of him half a century before the Minstrel sang :

> Off his gud dedis and manhad
> Gret gestis I hard say ar made,
> Bot sa mony, I trow noucht,
> As he in-till hys dayis wroucht.
> Quha all hys dedis of prys wald dyte
> Hym worthyt a gret buk to wryte.

It may therefore be supposed that Henry had sufficient latitude for additional episodes in the popular legends and " gret gestis" extant regarding the hero. Such a character was in much the same position to his chronicler as King Arthur and Charlemagne had been to the minstrels of the twelfth and thirteenth centuries, and was likely to find something of the same treatment.   Thus it is found that Henry's poem, besides much which was probable enough, and much which is proved to be historical by contemporary records, contains certain elements which could have no foundation in fact, but which were deemed indispensable to a hero of romance.

Of this sort is the episode of Wallace's interview with the English queen. Love as well as war was a necessary element of a minstrel's tale. It was not enough that the forces of the enemy should be defeated at Stirling Bridge and the great national purpose of the Liberator accomplished; it was necessary that that enemy should be personally humbled, and that even his wife's allegiance should become part of the spoils of the victor. Henry accordingly marches his hero south to the gates of London, where King Edward, driven to his last stronghold, and reduced to abject despair, is only saved at last by the intercession of his queen in the conqueror's camp. All this is romantic enough, and, like many other episodes throughout the poem, affords a sufficiently dramatic situation. But it is not to be read as history. Edward was at that particular time engaged in the French wars in Flanders, and though the Scottish forces, after clearing their enemies out of the northern kingdom, proceeded to lay utterly waste the provinces of Northumberland and Cumberland, it is not known that they passed further south. Other episodes of the poem as well, such as the opening battle of Biggar in which the hero is made to defeat Edward in person, are also obviously apocryphal; and the conclusion to which these compel the reader is that the composition as a whole must be regarded simply as a national romance founded upon popular tradition.

At the same time it may be as well to remember that within the last few decades several of Henry's episodes, such as the expedition of Wallace to France, formerly supposed to be fictitious, have been confirmed by discovery of authentic evidence.

For the actually ascertained facts of the hero's life the reader may be referred to the volume of "Documents Illustrative of Sir William Wallace, his Life and Times," edited for the Maitland Club by Mr. Robert Roger; and also to the admirable article on Wallace in the "Encyclopædia Britannica." From these it will be seen that though the Scottish Warden did not carry out all the enterprises attributed to him by Henry the Minstrel, he was by no means the mere robber and brigand which he was painted by Hemingford and the other English chroniclers of his time. It is significant of his enduring greatness that everywhere throughout Scotland to the present day there are places honoured for his memory. His name is, as Wordsworth says,

> To be found, like a wild flower,
> All over his dear Country.

In one respect at least the Minstrel's poem remains historically valuable. It affords an illustration of the state of national feeling in Henry's own time.

If from no more than a poetical point of view, however, the composition must continue to be regarded as a monumental work. There cannot but be something intrinsically worth study in a poem which, notwithstanding the disadvantage of its author's blindness from his birth, has remained uninterruptedly popular for centuries. Debarred by his infirmity from a field in which the Scottish poets especially excelled—the description of colour and natural scenery—the Minstrel displays a rude fire and energy and a power of realizing the telling points of action and situation beyond any of his predecessors. In a word, he possessed to a greater degree the modern spirit of romantic art. His hero, it is true, appears to lack the high-bred chivalry and polity of the Bruce as pourtrayed by Barbour, and displays at times an implacable ferocity which it is to be hoped did not belong to the actual character of the Liberator; while the Englishmen of the poem too commonly justify the description of Dr. Merry Ross—"mere poltroons or braggarts or felons." The temper of the Minstrel's work altogether is on a level with the temper of the common people of his time, from whom he sprang. But not the less is the *Wallace* equal to its great poetic purpose, bodying forth with broad master-strokes the tyranny which had burned its way to the passionate heart of the nation, and picturing the uprising of that national heart in the person of its early hero, uncertain in action at first, and with human desires and failings, till, stung by a crowning wrong, he grasps the weapons to his hands, hurls forth his defiance, and begins the struggle for liberty or death.

It is not impossible to understand the effect of these verses chanted to a warlike audience by the blind old Scottish Homer of the fifteenth century, recalling with vivid force, as they must have done, the heroic movement of the past, and awakening for a time again perhaps the embers of an ancient patriotism amid the miserable intestine bickerings of the reign of James the Third. The effect of the poem on a

Scottish mind, even in a later day, may be judged from the words of Robert Burns, who only knew the Minstrel's work through the paraphrase into modern Scottish by William Hamilton of Gilbertfield. " The story of Wallace," he says in his letter to Dr. Moore, " poured a tide of Scottish prejudice into my veins which will boil along there till the flood-gates of life shut in eternal rest."

SIR WILLIAM WALLACE.

[The poem opens with a complaint that the Scots forget their noble ancestors, and do honour only to their enemies. The descent of Wallace is traced and Edward's oppression briefly recounted. As a youth visiting Dundee, Wallace is insulted by the son of Selby the governor, and slays him in the street. The house in which he takes refuge is searched, but, dressed as a maid at the spinning-wheel, the hero is overlooked. Flying home to Ellerslie he finds his father and elder brother slain ; and his mother, fearful for the safety of her remaining son, sends him to his uncle, Sir Richard Wallace of Ricardton. But presently, fishing one day in Irvine Water, he is attacked by some English men-at-arms, who attempt to carry off his fish, and he slays three of them. Visiting Ayr, and venturing to defend his uncle's servant, he is overpowered and cast into prison, but soon, taken for dead, is thrown over the castle wall. His nurse begs his body and carries him to her house, where he is revived with milk from her daughter's breast. Thomas the Rhymer, staying at hand with the minister, on hearing this news, prophesies the great future of Wallace. Gathering some friends, the hero waylays Lord Percy's succours at Loudon Hill, routs them, and slays their leader Fenwick, who had been the elder Wallace's murderer. Known presently as a champion of the Scottish cause, Wallace finds himself at the head of a considerable band of followers, and makes his way northwards, taking Gargunnock Peel and the castle of Kincleven. At Perth, in an amorous adventure, he narrowly escapes capture.]

A Love Adventure.

HAN Wallace said he wald go to the toun,
Arayit him weill in-till a preistlik goun ;
In Sanct Jhonstoun* disgysyt can he fair,
Till this woman the quhilk I spak of ayr[1].

[1] whom I spake of formerly.

* The ancient name of Perth.

Off his presence scho rycht reiosit was;

¹ afraid. And sor adred¹ how he away suld pass.

He soiornyt thar fra nowne was of the day

Quhill ner the nycht, or that he went away.

² made appoint-
ment with. He trystyt² hyr quhen he wald cum agayne,

On the thrid day; than was scho wondyr fayne.

³ went. Yhett he was seyn with enemyss as he yeid³;

To Schyr Garraid thai tald off all his deid,

⁴ been revenged. And to Butler, that wald haiff wrokyn beyne⁴.

⁵ beautiful. Than thai gart tak that woman brycht and scheyne⁵,

Accusyt hir sar of resset in that cas.

⁶ Many times. Feyll syis⁶ scho suour that scho knew nocht Wallas.

⁷ know. Than Butler said, "We wait⁷ weyle it was he;

And bot thou tell, in bayle fyre sall thou de.

Giff thou will help to bryng yon rebell doune

We sall the mak a lady off renoun."

Thai gaiff till hyr baith gold and siluer brycht;

And said scho suld be weddyt with ane knycht

⁸ without. Quham scho desirit, that was but⁸ mariage.

Thus tempt thai hir, throu consaill and gret wage,

That scho thaim tald quhat tyme he wald be thar.

Than war thai glad; for thai desirit no mar

Off all Scotland, bot Wallace at thair will.

Thus ordaynyt thai this poyntment to fullfill.

⁹ made ready. Feyle men off armes thai graithit⁹ hastelye

¹⁰ gates. To kepe the yettis¹⁰, wicht Wallas till aspye.

At the set trist he entrit in the toune,

¹¹ knowing. Wittand¹¹ no-thing of all this falss tresoune.

¹² without more
delay. Till hir chawmer he went but mair abaid¹².

Scho welcummyt him, and full gret plesance maid.

¹³ readily. Quhat at thai wrocht I can nocht graithly¹³ say;

Rycht wnperfyt I am of Venus play:
Bot hastelye he graithit him to gang.
Than scho him tuk, and speryt giff he thocht lang[1];   [1] asked if he felt weary.
Scho askit him that nycht with hir to bid.
Sone he said, "Nay, for chance that may betide;
My men ar left all at mysrewill for me.
I may nocht sleipe this nycht quhill I thaim se."
Than wepyt scho, and said full oft, "Allace
That I was maide, wa worthe the coursit cas[2]!   [2] woe befall the accursed chance.
Now haiff I lost the best man leiffand is.
O feble mynd, to do so foull a myss[3]!   [3] fault.
O waryit witt, wykkyt and wariance[4],   [4] O cursed craft and unjust adjuring.
That me has brocht in-to this myschefull[5] chance!   [5] unhappy.
Allace," scho said, "in warld that I was wrocht,
Giff all this payne on my-self mycht be brocht!
I haiff seruit to be brynt in a gleid[6]."   [6] a bright fire.
Quhen Wallace saw scho ner of witt couth weid[7],   [7] with thought would fever.
In his armes he caucht hir sobrely,
And said, "Der hart, quha has mysdoyne ocht, I?"
"Nay, I," quoth scho, "has falslye wrocht this trayn.
I haiff you sald; rycht now yhe will be slayn."
Scho tauld [to] him hir tresoun till ane end,
As I haiff said; quhat nedis mair legend?
At hir he speryt giff scho forthocht it sar[8].   [8] repented it sore.
"Wa, ya," scho said, "and sall do euirmar.
My waryed werd[9] in warld I mon fullfill;   [9] accursed fate.
To mend this myss I wald byrne on a hill."
He comfort hir, and baide hir haiff no dreide,
"I will," he said, "haiff sumpart off thi weid."
Hir gowne he tuk on hym, and courches als[10].   [10] kerchief also.
"Will God, I sall eschape this tresoune fals.

I the forgyff." With-outyn wordis mair
He kissyt hyr, syne tuk his leiff to fayr.
Hys burly brand that helpyt him offt in neid,
Rycht priẅalye he hid it wndyr that weid.

1 nearest.　To the south yett the gaynest[1] way he drew;
Quhar that he fand off armyt men enew.
To thaim he tald, dissemblyt [in] contenance;
" To the chawmer, quhar he was vpon chance,
Speid fast," he said, " Wallace is lokit in."
Fra him thai socht with-outyn noyis or dyn
To that sammyn houss; about thai can thaim cast.
Out at the yett [than] Wallas gat full fast,
Rycht glaid in hart; quhen that he was with-out

2 swift.　Rycht fast he yeide, a stour[2] pais and a stout.
Twa him beheld, and said, " We will go se;
A stalwart queyne, forsuth, yon semyss to be."
Him thai folowit throwe the South Ynche thai twa.
Quhen Wallace saw with thaim thar come na ma
Agayne he turnede, and has the formast slayn.
The tothir fled; than Wallas, with gret mayn,
Vpon the hed with his suerd has him tayne;
Left thaim bathe dede, syne to the strenth is gayne.
His men he gat, rycht glaid quhen thai him saw;

3 caused.　Till thair defens in haist he gart[3] thaim draw;
Deuoydyde him sone of the womannys weid:

4 extremedanger. Thus chapyt he out of that felloun dreid[4].

An Apparition in Gask Hall.

[As the little Scottish company, pursued by the English garrison of Perth with a bloodhound, are making for the Forest of Gask, Fawdoun, a suspected traitor, declares he can go no further. Wallace, to prevent treachery, strikes off his head. The hound stops at the blood, and while the stars are shining the fugitives reach their retreat.]

As Wallace thus in the thik forrest socht,
Threttene war left with him, no ma had he.
In the Gask hall thair lugyng haif thai tayne;
Fyr gat thai sone, bot meyt than had thai nane.
Twa scheipe thai tuk besid thaim of a fauld,
Ordanyt to soupe in-to that sembly hauld.
Graithit in haist sum fude for thaim to dycht[1],   [1] prepare.
So hard thai blaw rude hornys wpon hycht[2].   [2] on high.
Twa sende he furth to luk quhat it mycht be.
Thai baid rycht lang, and no tithingis herd he,
Bot boustous[3] noyis so brymly[4] blowand fast.   [3] tremendous.
                                                    [4] fiercely.
So othir twa in-to the woode furth past.
Nane come agayne, bot boustously can blaw.
In-to gret ire he send thaim furth on raw[5].   [5] in rank.
Quhen he allayne Wallace was lewyt thar
The awfull blast aboundyt mekill mayr[6].   [6] much more.
Than trowit he weill thai had his lugyng seyne;
His suerd he drew of nobill mettall keyne,
Syn furth he went quhar at he hard the horne.
With-out the dur Fawdoun was him beforn,
As till his sycht, his awne hed in his hand.
A croys he maid quhen he saw him so stand.
At Wallace in the hed he swaket[7] thar;   [7] hurled.
And he in haist sone hynt[8] [it] by the hair,   [8] laid hold of.

Syne out agayne at him he couth it cast.

In-till his hart he was gretlye agast.

Rycht weill he trowit that was no spreit of man;

1 that such.   It was sum dewill at sic[1] malice began.

2 advantage.   He wyst no waill[2] thar langar for to bide;

Vp throuch the hall thus wicht Wallace can glid,

3 rent in twain.   Till a closs stair; the burdis raiff in twyne[3],

4 dwelling.   Fyftene fute large he lap out of that in[4].

Wp the wattir sodeynlye he couth fair.

5 glanced.   Agayne he blent[5] quhat perance he saw thair.

Him thocht he saw Faudoun, that hugly syr;

That haill hall he had set in a fyr;

A gret raftre he had in-till his hand.

Wallace as than no langar walde he stand.

Off his gud men full gret meruaill had he,

6 lost.   How thai war tynt[6] throuch his feyle[7] fantasé.
7 strong.
8 true.   Traistis rycht weill all this was suth[8] in deide,

9 Although.   Supposs[9] that it no poynt be of the creide.

[He escapes through his enemies with great difficulty, fighting
nearly all the way, and, swimming the Forth at Cambuskenneth,
finds refuge in the Torwood. He sends back a woman to survey
the scene of the previous night, and he is joined by his uncle.]

In the Torwode thai lugyt all that nycht,

Quhill the woman that Wallace north had send

Retornd agayne, and tald him till ane end

Quhat Inglissmen in the way scho fand dede.

10 Many.   Feyll[10] was fallyn fey[11] in mony syndry stede;
11 at point of
    death.   The hors scho saw that Wallace had berefft,

And the Gask hall standand as it was left,

12 stirred.   With-out harme, nocht sterd[12] off it a stane;

Bot off his men gud tithingis scho gat nane.

[Visiting Lanark, Wallace becomes enamoured of a young lady, the orphan daughter of Hew Braidfute of Lamington, but defers marriage till Scotland shall be free. Shortly afterwards, while the hero and his men are attending mass at Lochmaben, the English cut the tails from their horses. In the fight that ensues the English are defeated, and, Wallace being joined by Sir John the Graham, Lochmaben and Crawford castles are taken. A little later, seized with resistless love-longing, Wallace weds Marion Braidfute, and they live together until a daughter is born. But in 1297, for aiding her husband's escape from a street brawl in Lanark, the lady is put to death. At the news, Wallace is overwhelmed with grief, but presently vows implacable vengeance. He storms Lanark at midnight ; puts his enemies to the sword, and shortly finds himself at the head of an army. So serious appears the rising that King Edward himself with a great force comes to Scotland. He is defeated, however, in two great battles at Biggar, and in consequence at " Forest Kyrk" Wallace is chosen Warden of the country. Edward seeks peace, and a truce of a year is agreed on. In two months this truce is broken by English treachery at the terrible " Barns of Ayr," where eighteen score Scottish gentlemen, invited to a justice ayre, and admitted two by two, are hanged to the rafters. Wallace, who meanwhile has seen a vision of his future in a dream in Monkton Kirk, is only saved by a chance delay and the warning of a woman. He avenges the treachery by burning five thousand English in their inns at Ayr on the same night. This was at ten at night. By nine next morning he is in Glasgow, where a similar justice ayre is appointed to be held, and routs Earl Percy and Bishop Beck. Called then to the help of Campbell of Lochow, he defeats and slays Macfadyen, Edward's creature in the west, in a pass under Ben More. Meanwhile Malcolm, Earl of Lennox, has taken Stirling for Wallace, and the latter, after holding a counsel at Ardchattan, captures Perth and Dunottar.]

The Battle of Stirling Bridge.

[Wallace burns a hundred English ships at Aberdeen, and all the north falls to his hand. He is besieging Dundee when, alarmed at the news, King Edward sends a large force into Scotland under Warenne and Cressingham with orders to wait his own coming at Stirling.]

Thar mustir than was awfull for to se.
Off fechtand men thousandis thai war sexté
To Stirlyng past, or thai likit to bid.

To erll Malcome a sege thai laid that tid,
And thocht to kep the commaund off thar king.
Bot gud Wallace wrocht for ane-othir thing.
Dundé he left, and maid a gud chyftane,
With twa thousand, to kepe that hous off stayne,
Off Angwis men and duellaris off Dundé;
The samyn nycht till Sanct Jhonstoun went he.
Apon the morn till Schirreff-mur he raid;
And thar a quhill in gud aray thai baid.

^x capable.

Schir Jhon the Grayme, and Ramsay that was wicht¹,
He said to thaim, "This is my purpos rycht;

² Too much.

Our mekill² it is to proffer thaim battaill

³ advantage.

Apon a playne feild; bot we haiff sum aẅaill³."
Schir Jhon the Grayme said, 'We haiff wndirtayn,
With less power, sic thing that weill is gayn.'
Than Wallace said, "Quhar sic thing cummys off
        neid,
We suld thank God that makis ws for to speid.
Bot ner the bryg my purpos is to be,
And wyrk for thaim sum suttell jeperté."
Ramsay ansuerd, 'The brig we may kepe weill;

⁴ knowledge.

Off way about Sotheroun has litill feill⁴.'
Wallace sent Jop the battaill for to set,

⁵ without fail.

The Twysday next to fecht with-outyn let⁵.
On Setterday on to the bryg thai raid,

⁶ compactly.

Off gud playne burd was weill and junctly⁶ maid;

⁷ Caused watches to see to it.

Gert wachis wait⁷ that nane suld fra thaim pass.
A wricht he tuk, the suttellast at thar was,
And ordand him to saw the burd in twa
Be the myd streit, that nane mycht our it ga;

⁸ jointed bands, *i.e.*, strong hinges.

On charnaill bandis⁸ nald it full fast and sone,

Syne fyld[1] with clay as na-thing had beyne done. [1] Afterwards soiled.
The tothir end he ordand for to be,
How it suld stand on thre rowaris[2] off tre, [2] bolts.
Quhen ane war out, that the laiff doun suld fall.
Him-selff wndyr he ordand thar with-all,
Bownd on the trest[3] in a creddill to sit, [3] beam, trestle.
To lous the pyne quhen Wallace leit him witt.
Bot with a horn, quhen it was tyme to be,
In all the ost suld no man blaw bot he.

The day approchit off the gret battaill;
The Inglismen for power wald nocht faill.
Ay sex thai war agayne ane off Wallace;
Fyfty thousand maid thaim to battaill place.
The ramaynand baid at the castell still;
Baithe feild and hous thai thocht to tak at will.
The worthi Scottis, apon the tothir side,
The playne feild tuk, on fute maid thaim to bid.
Hew Kertyngayme the wantgard ledis he,
With twenty thousand off likly men to se.
Thretty thousand the erll off Waran had;
Bot he did than as the wysman him bad;
All the fyrst ost befor him our was send[4]. [4] was sent over.
Sum Scottis men that weill the maner kend[5] [5] knew.
Bade Wallace blaw, and said thai war enew.
He haistyt nocht, bot sadly[6] couth persew, [6] wisely, firmly.
Quhill Warans ost thik on the bryg he saw.
Fra Jop the horn he hyntyt and couth blaw
Sa asprely[7], and warned gud Jhon Wricht. [7] shrilly.
The rowar out he straik with gret slycht;
The laiff[8] yeid doun, quhen the pynnys out gais. [8] The remainder.

A hidwys cry amang the peple rais;
Bathe hors and men in-to the wattir fell.
The hardy Scottis, that wald na langar duell,
Set on the laiff with strakis sad and sar,

[1] Assured of them that were over. Off thaim thar our as than souerit[1] thai war.

[2] At the forefront they essayed. At the forbreist thai prewit[2] hardely,

Wallace and Grayme, Boid, Ramsay, and Lundy,

[3] struggle. All in the stour[3] fast fechtand face to face.

The Sotheron ost bak rerit off that place

[4] That. At[4] thai fyrst tuk, fyve akyr breid and mar.

Wallace on fute a gret scharp sper he bar;
Amang the thikest off the press he gais.
On Kertyngaym a straik chosyn he hais

[5] corselet. In the byrnes[5], that polyst was full brycht.

[6] sharp, penetrating. The punyeand[6] hed the plattis persyt rycht,

Throuch the body stekit him but reskew;

[7] Boldly. [8] done. Derffly[7] to dede that chyftane was adew[8].

Baithe man and hors at that strak he bar doun.

[9] prepared. The Inglis ost quhilk war in battaill boun[9],

Comfort thai lost quhen thair chyftayne was slayn;
And mony ane to fle began in playne.
Yeit worthi men baid still in-to the sted,
Quhill ten thousand was brocht on-to thair dede.
Than fled the laiff, and mycht no langar bid;
Succour thai socht on mony diuers sid,
Sum est, sum west, and sum fled to the north.

[10] Over seven thousand at once splashed. Sewyn thousand large at anys flottryt[10] in Forth,

Plungyt the depe, and drownd with-out mercye;

[11] immense following. Nayne left on lyff off all that feill menyhe[11].

[12] avail, consequence. Off Wallace ost na man was slayne off waill[12],

Bot Andrew Murray, in-to that strang battaill.

The south part than, saw at thar men was tynt[1],   [1] lost.
Als fersly fled as fyr dois off the flynt.
The place thai left, castell, and Stirlyng toune;
Towart Dunbar in gret haist maid thaim boune.

Quhen Wallace ost had won that feild throuch mycht,
Tuk wp the bryg, and loussit gud Jhone Wricht;
On the flearis syne folowed wondyr fast.
Erll Malcom als out off the castell past,
With Lennox men, to stuff[2] the chace gud speid.   [2] supply.
Ay be the way thai gert feill[3] Sotheroun bleid;   [3] caused many.
In the Torwod thai gert full mony de.
The erll off Waran, that can full fersly fle,
With Corspatrik, that graithly[4] was his gyd,   [4] readily.
On changit hors throuch-out the land thai rid,
Strawcht to Dunbar; bot few with thaim thai led.
Mony was slayne our sleuthfully at fled.
The Scottis hors that had rown wondyr lang,
Mony gaiff our, that mycht no forthyr gang.
Wallace and Grayme euir to-giddyr baid;
At Hathyntoun full gret slauchtir thai maid
Off Inglismen, quhen thair hors tyryt had.
Quhen Ramsay come gud Wallace was full glad;
With him was Boid, and Richard off Lundy,
Thre thousand haill[5] was off gud chewalry;   [5] whole, quite.
And Adam als Wallace off Ricardtoune,
With erll Malcome, thai fand at Hathyntoune.
The Scottis men on slauchtir taryt was[6],   [6] were restrained.
Quhill to Dunbar the twa chyftanys couth pass,
Full sitfully[7], for thar gret contrar cas[8].   [7] sorrowfully.
   [8] hap.
Wallace folowed till thai gat in that place.

Off thair best men, and Kertyngaym off renoune,
Twenty thousand was dede but redemptioune.
Besyd Beltoun Wallace raturnd agayn;
To folow mar as than was bot in ẅayn.

Wallace and the Queen of England.

[Wallace summons a parliament at Perth, but Corspatrick,
Earl of March, refuses to attend, flouting the Warden as a "king
of Kyle." In consequence Wallace at Dunbar attacks and routs
the haughty noble. The latter is reinforced by a large army from
England under Bruce and Bishop Beck, but this also is discom-
fited by the enterprise of the Scots, though it grieves the leader
to find his king fighting among the national enemies. To recoup
the nation's losses Wallace next determines on an invasion of
England, and the poet makes him march south, burning and
slaying, and continually evaded by the English king, as far as
St. Albans. The English barons determine to sue for peace,
but, mindful of the ruthlessness of the Warden, no herald will
venture to his camp. At last the queen offers to go. The
Scottish leader wakens early in his tent.]

The mery day sprang fra the oryent,
With bemys brycht enlumynyt the occident.
Eftir Titan, Phebus wp rysyt fayr,
Heich in the sper the signes maid declayr.
Zepherus began his morow cours,

¹ rises again.
The swete ẅapour thus fra the ground resours[1].

² humble, gentle.
³ descends.
The humyll[2] breyth doun fra the heẅyn aẅaill[3],

In euery meide, bathe fyrth, forrest, and daill;

⁴ note.
The cler rede[4] amang the rochis rang
Throuch greyn branchis quhar byrdis blythly sang
With joyus ẅoice in heẅynly armony.
Than Wallace thocht it was no tyme to ly;
He croyssit him, syne sodeynli wp rais;

To tak the ayr out off his palyon¹ gais.

Maister Jhon Blar was redy to rawess;

In gud entent syne bownyt to the mess².

Quhen it was done Wallace can him aray³

In his armour quhilk gudly was and gay.

His schenand schoys⁴ that burnyst was full beyn⁵,

His leg harnes he clappyt on so clene;

Pullane greis⁶ he braissit on full fast;

A closs byrny with mony sekyr⁷ clasp;

Breyst-plait, brasaris⁸, that worthy was in wer.

Besid him furth Jop couth his basnet ber.

His glytterand glowis grawin on athir sid,

He semyt weill in battaill till abid.

His gud gyrdyll, and syne his burly brand,

A staff off steyll he gryppyt in his hand.

The ost him blyst, and prayit God off his grace

Him to conwoy fra all mystymyt cace⁹.

Adam Wallace and Boid furth with him yeid

By a reuir, throu-out a floryst meid.

And as thai walk atour¹⁰ the feyldis greyn,

Out off the south thai saw quhar at the queyn

Towart the ost come ridand sobyrly,

And fyfty ladyis was in hyr cumpany,

Wallyt¹¹ off wit and demyt¹² off renoun,

Sum wedowis war, and sum off religioun;

And sewyn preistis that entrit war in age.

Wallace to sic¹³ did neuir gret owtrage,

Bot gyff till him thai maid a gret offens.

Thus prochyt thai on towart thar presens.

At the palyoun quhar thai the lyoun saw

To ground thai lycht, and syne on kneis can faw;

¹ pavilion.

² make ready for the mass.

³ began to array himself.

⁴ shining shoon.
⁵ richly.

⁶ Battle greaves.

⁷ sure.

⁸ vambraces.

⁹ untimely hap.

¹⁰ across.

¹¹ Chosen.
¹² judged.

¹³ such.

Prayand for pece thai cry with petous cher.

Erll Malcom said, " Our chyftayn is nocht her."

He bad hyr rys, and said it was nocht rycht,

¹ serving wight. A queyn on kneis till ony lavar wycht¹.

Wp by the hand the gud erll has hyr tayn ;

Atour the bent to Wallace ar thai gayn.

Quhen scho him saw scho wald haiff knelyt doune ;

In armys sone he caucht this queyn with croun,

And kyssyt hyr with-outyn wordis mor ;

Sa dyd he neuir to na Sotheron befor.

² may. " Madem," he said, " rycht welcum mot² ye be ;

How plessis yow our ostyng for to se ?"

[The Scots lords and English ladies dine together, and after-
wards the queen sues for peace. All her arguments, however,
are in vain, and when Wallace recounts at length the woes of
Scotland and his own wrongs the queen herself weeps for pity.]

³ fair talk helped   The queyn fand weyll langage no-thing hyr bet³ ;
her nothing.

⁴ overcome. Scho trowit with gold that he mycht be our-set⁴.

Thre thousand pound off fynest gold so red

Scho gert be brocht to Wallace in that sted.

" Madeym," he said, " na sic tribut we craiff.

A-nothir mendis we wald off Ingland haiff,

Or we raturn fra this regioun agayn,

Off your fals blud that has our elderis slayn.

⁵ realm. For all the gold and ryches ye in ryng⁵,

Ye get no pess, but desir off your king."

Quhen scho saw weill, gold mycht hyr nocht releiff,

Sum part in sport scho thoucht him for to preiff.

⁶ called. ' Wallace,' scho said, ' yhe war clepyt⁶ my luff.

⁷ courageously. Mor baundounly⁷ I maid me for to pruff,

Traistand tharfor your rancour for to slak.

Me-think ye suld do sum-thing for my saik.'
Rycht wysly he maid ansuer to the queyn.
"Madem," he said, "and verité war seyn
That ye me luffyt, I awcht[1] yow luff agayn.   [1] owe.
Thir wordis all ar no-thing bot in wayn.
Sic luff as that is nothing till awance,
To tak a lak[2], and syne get no plesance.   [2] reproach.
In spech off luff suttell ye Sotheroun ar;
Ye can ws mok, suppos ye se no mar."
'In London,' scho said, 'for yow I sufferyt blaym;
Our consall als will lauch quhen we cum haym.
So may thai say, wemen ar fers[3] off thocht   [3] quick, eager.
To sek frendschip, and syne can get rycht nocht!'
"Madem," he said, "we wait[4] how ye ar send;   [4] understand.
Yhe trow we haiff bot litill for to spend.
Fyrst with your gold, for ye ar rych and wys[5],   [5] crafty.
Yhe wald ws blynd, sen Scottis ar so nys[6]:   [6] uncrafty.
Syn plesand wordis off yow and ladyis fayr,
As quha suld dryff the byrdis till a swar[7]   [7] snare.
With the small pype, for it most fresche will call.
Madem, as yit ye ma nocht tempt ws all.
Gret part off gud is left amang our kyn;
In Ingland als we fynd enewch to wyn."
Abayssyt[8] scho was to mak ansuer him till.   [8] At a loss.
'Der schyr,' scho said, 'sen this is at your will;
Wer or pess, quhat-so yow likis best,
Lat your hye witt and gud consaill degest[9].'   [9] deliberate.
"Madem," he said, "now sall ye wndirstand
The resoune quhy that I will mak na band.
With yow, ladyis, I can na trewis bynd;
For your fals king her-eftir sone wald fynd,

Quhen he saw tyme, to brek it at his will,
And playnly say he grantyt nocht thartill.
Than had we nayn bot ladyis to repruff.
That sall he nocht, be God that is abuff.
Vpon wemen I will na wer begyn;
On you in faith no worschip is to wyn.
All the haill pass apon him-selff he sall tak,
Off pees or wer quhat hapnyt we to mak."
The queyn grantyt his ansuer sufficient;

¹ the remainder.   So dyd the layff[1] in place that was present.
His delyuerance thai held off gret awaill,
² potent.   And stark[2] enewch to schaw to thair consaill.
Wa was the qweyn hyr trawaill helpyt nocht.
The gold scho tuk, that thai had with hyr brocht;
On-to the ost rycht frely scho it gayff
Till euirylk man that likyt for till haiff.
Till menstraillis, harroldis, scho delt haboundanlé,
Besekand thaim hyr frend at thai wald be.
Quhen Wallace saw the fredom off the queyn,
Sadly he said, "The suth weyll has beyn seyn,
Wemen may tempt the wysest at is wrocht.

3 gentlehood.   Your gret gentrice[3] it sall neuir be for nocht.
We [yow] assure our ost sall mwff na-thing
Quhyll tym ye may send message fra your king.
Gyff it be sa at he accord and we,
Than for your saik it sall the bettir be.
Your harroldys als sall saiffly cum and ga;

4 no more.   For your fredom we sall trowbill na ma[4]."
5 times.   Scho thankit him off his grant mony sys[5],
And all the ladyis apon a gudly wys.
Glaidly thai drank, the queyn and gud Wallace,

Thir ladyis als and lordis in that place.
Hyr lcyff ocho tuk with out langar abaid;
Fyve myile that nycht south till a nonry raid.
Apon the morn till London passit thai,
In Westmenster, quhar at the consaill lay.

The Red Reiver.

[Peace is presently arranged, Edward giving up all Scottish fortresses and prisoners. Three years later, the affairs of all Scotland having been set in order, Wallace is invited by the French king to visit France, and leaving Sir James Stewart at the head of the government, he sets sail. At sea his vessel is attacked by Longueville, the Red Reiver, with sixteen ships; but by his personal address and strength, seizing the pirate captain as he leaps on board, Wallace captures the whole fleet.]

Wallace desyryt to talk mor with this man.
Sadly he sperd[1], "Off quhat land was thou born?"   [1] Seriously he asked.
'Off France,' quoth he, 'and my eldris beforn;
And thar we had sumpart off heretage:
Yet fers fortoun thus brocht me in a rage.'
Wallace sperd, "How com thow to this lyff?"
'Forsuth,' he said, 'bot throw a sudan stryff.
So hapnyt me in-to the kingis presens
Our raklesly to do our gret offens.
A nobill man off gud fame and renoun
That throw my deid was put to confusioun
Dede off a straik; quhat nedis wordis mor?
All helpyt nocht, thocht I repentyt full sor.
Throw freyndys off the court I chapyt[2] off that place,   [2] escaped.
And neuir sen syn[3] couth get the kingis grace.   [3] since then.
For my saik mony off my kyn gert thai de.

And quhen I saw it mycht no bettir be,
Bot leyff the land that me behuffyt o neid,

¹ to Bordeaux I went.

Apon a day to Burdeous I yeid[1].
Ane Inglis schip so gat I on a nycht,

² expeditiously was prepared.

For sey lawbour that ernystfully was dycht[2].

³ gathered.

To me thar semblyt[3] misdoaris, and weill mo;
And in schort tym we multiplyit so
That thar wes few our power mycht withstand.

⁴ reigned long.

In tyranry thus haiff we rongyn lang[4].
This sexten yer I haiff beyn on the se,
And doyn gret harm; tharfor full wa is me.
I savit nayn, for gold nor gret ransoun,
Bot slew and drownyt in-to the se adoun.
Faẅour I did till folk off syndry land;
Bot Franchmen no frendschip with me fand,
Thai gat no grace als fer as I mycht ryng.

⁵ called.

Als on the se I clypyt[5] was a king.
Now se I weyll that my fortoun is went,
Vincust with ane; that gerris me sair rapent.
Quha wald haiff said, this sammyn day at morn,
I suld with ane thus lychtly doun be born,

⁶ scorn.

In gret hething[6] my men it wald haiff tayne.

⁷ overwhelmed.

My-selff trowit till [haiff] machit[7] mony ane,
Bot I haiff found the werray playn contrar.
Her I gyff our roubry for euirmar;
In sic mysrewll I sall neuir armes ber,

⁸ use, manner.

Bot gyff it be in honest oys[8] to wer.
Now haiff I told part off my blyss and payn;

⁹ show.

For Goddis saik sum kyndnes kyth[9] agayn.
My hart will brek bot I wyt quhat thou be

¹⁰ abated, reduced.

Thus outrageously that has rabutyt[10] me.

For weill I wend[1] that leyffand had beyn non   [1] deemed.
Be fors off strenth mycht me as presoner ton
Except Wallace, that has rademyt Scotland,
The best is callyt this day beltyt with brand.
In-till his wer war worschip for to wak[2],   [2] travel.
As now in warld I trow he has no mak[3].'   [3] peer.
Tharat he smylit, and said; "Frend, weill may be,
Scotland had mystir[4] off mony sic as he.   [4] need.
Quhat is thi naym? tell me; so haiff thow seill[5]!"   [5] happiness.
'Forsuth,' he said, 'Thomas of Longaweill.'
"Weyll bruk[6] thow it! all thus stentis[7] our stryff: [6] enjoy.
Schaip[8] to pleyss God in mendyng off thi lyff.   [7] stays.
    [8] Endeavour.
Thi faithfull freynd my-selff thinkis to be;
And als my nayme I sall sone tell to the.
For chans off wer thou suld no murnyng mak;
As werd[9] will wyrk thi fortoun mon[10] thou tak.   [9] fate.
    [10] must.
I am that man that you awanss so hie,
And bot schort tym sen I come to the se.
Off Scotland born, my rycht name is Wallace."
On kneis he fell, and thankit God of grace;
'I dar awow that yoldyn is my hand
To the best man that beltis him with brand.
Forsuth,' he said, 'this blythis me mekill mor
Than off floryng ye gaiff me sexty scor.'
Wallace ansuerd; "Sen thou art her throw chance,
My purpos is, be this wiage, in France;
And to the king sen I am boun to pass,
To my reward thi pees I think to as."
'Pes I wald haiff [fane] off my rychtwis king;
And no langar in-to that realm to ryng[11],   [11] reign.
Than to tak leyff, and cum off it agayn.

In thi seruice I think for to ramayn.'
" Seruice," he said, " Thomas, that may nocht be,
Bot gud frendschip, as I desir off the."
Gart¹ draw the wyn, and ilk man mery maid ;
Be this the schippis was in the Rochell raid.

   The rede blasonys thai had born in-to wer ;
The toun was sone in-till a sudane fer.
The Rede Reiffar thai saw was at thair hand,
The quhilk throu strenth mycht nayn agayne him
    stand.
Sum schippis fled, and sum the land has tayn,
Clariownys blew, and trumpattis mony ane.
Quhen Wallace saw the pepill was on ster²
He gaiff commaund na schip suld ner apper,
Bot his awin barge in-to the haẅyn gart draw.
The folk was fayn quhen thai that senye³ saw ;
Rycht weyll thai knew in gold the rede lioun,
Leit wp the port rasauit him in the toun,
And sufferyt thaim, for all that he had brocht.
The rede naẅyn in-to the haẅyn thai socht ;
On land thai went, quhar thai likit to pass.
Rycht few thar wyst quhat Scottisman Wallace was ;
Bot weyll thai thocht he was a gudly man,
And honouryt him in all the craft thai can.

[Wallace carries Longueville in his suite to the French court.]

   Sone eftir meit the king to parlour went,
With gudly lordis ; thar Wallace was present.
Than commound thai off mony syndry thing ;
To spek with him gret desyr had the king.

¹ Caused.

² in commotion.

³ ensign.

At him he speryt off wer the gouernance.
He ansuerd him with manly contenance
Till euery poynt, als fer as he had feill[1],   [1] knowledge.
In Latyn tong rycht naturaly and weill.
The king consauit sone throu his hie knawlage
Quhat wermen oysyt be reyff[2] in thar passage.   [2] What men of
                                                                 war were wont
In-till his mynd the Rede Reiffar than was;   by robbery (to
Merẅell he had how he leit Wallace pass.   do).
Till him he said, "Ye war sum-thing to blaym;
Ye mycht haiff send, be our harrold fra haym,
Eftir power to bryng yow throu the se."
'God thank yow, schyr, tharoff ynewch had we.
Feill[3] men may pass quhar thai fynd na perell;   [3] Many.
Rycht few may kep quhar nayn is to assail.'
"Wallace," he said, "tharoff merẅell haiff I;
A tyran ryngis in ire full cruelly
Apon the se, that gret sorow has wrocht;
Mycht we him get, it suld not be for nocht.
Born off this land, a natyff man to me;
Tharfor on ws the grettar harme dois he."
Than Thomas quok, and changyt contenans;
He hard the king his eẅill deidis aẅans.
Wallace beheld, and fenyeit in a part[4];   [4] feigned a part.
'Forsuth,' he said, 'we fand nane in that art
That proffryt ws sic wnkyndlynes.
Bot with your leiff I spek in haymlynes,
Trow ye be sycht ye couth that squier knaw?'
"Full lang it war sen tym that I him saw.
Bot thir wordis off him ar bot in ẅayn;
Or he com her rycht gud men will be slayn."
Than Wallace said, 'Her I haiff brocht with me,

Off likly men that was in our countré :
Quhilk off all thir wald ye call him most lik ?'

¹ glanced.
² potent.
³ Examined.

Amang thaim blent¹ that ryoll roy most ryk²,
Wesyit³ thaim weill, bathe statur and curage,
Maner, makdome, thar fassoun and thar wesage.
Sadly he said, awysit sobyrly,
"That largest man, quhilk standis next yow by,
Wald I call him, be makdome to dewice.
Thir ar no thing bot wordis off office."
Befor the king on kneis fell gud Wallace :
'O ryoll roy, off hie honour and grace,
With waist wordis I will nocht yow trawaill ;
Now I will spek sum-thing for myn awaill.

⁴ native, *lit.*
   bairnhood.
⁵ injury.

Our barnat⁴ land has beyn our-set with wer,
With Saxonis blud that dois ws mekill der⁵,
Slayn our eldris, distroyit our rychtwys blud,
Waistyt our realm off gold and othir gud.
And ye ar her, in mycht and ryolté,
Yow suld haiff ey till our aduersité,
And ws support, throu kyndnes off the band
Quhilk is conserwyt betuix yow and Scotland.
As I am her, at your charge, for plesance,

⁶ way of life.
⁷ acquiring.

My lyflat⁶ is bot honest chewysance⁷.
Flour off realmys forsuth is this regioun ;

⁸ guerdon.

To my reward I wald haiff gret gardoun⁸.'
"Wallace," he said, "now ask what ye wald haiff.
Gud gold or land sall nocht be lang to craiff."
Wallace ansuerd, 'So ye it grant to me,
Quhat I wald haiff it sall sone chosyn be.'
"Quhat-euir yhe ask that is in this regioun,
Ye sall it haiff, except my wyff and croun."

He thankit hym off his gret kyndlynes.
' My reward all sall be askyng off grace,
Pees to this man I broucht with me throu chans.
Her I quytcleym¹ all othir gyfftis in Frans.   ¹ quit claim of.
This samyn is he, gyff ye knaw him weill,
That we off spak, Thomas off Longaẅeill.
Be rygour ye desyryt he suld be slayn ;
I him restor in-to your grace agayn.
Rasaiff him fayr, as liege man off your land.'

The king marẅeld, and couth in study stand ;
Perfytly knew that it was Longaẅeill ;
He him forgaiff his trespas euirilkdeill²,   ² every whit.
Bot for his saik that had him hydder brocht ;
For gold or land ellis he gat it nocht.
" Wallace," he said, " I had leuir³ off gud land   ³ leifer, rather.
Thre hundreth pund haiff sesyt⁴ in thi hand.   ⁴ paid.
That I haiff said sall be grantyt in plain ;
Her I restor Thomas to pes agayn,
Derer to me than euir he was befor,
All for your saik, thocht it war mekill mor."

Quhen Thomas was restoryt to his rycht
Off hys awin hand the king has maid him knycht.
Eftir he gaiff stayt to his nerrest ayr,
And maid him-selff with Wallace for to fayr.
Thus he was brocht fra naym off reyff, throu cace,
Be sudand chans off him and wicht Wallace.

The Taking of Lochleven.

[While Wallace assists the French in their wars in Guyenne, news of his deeds reaches the English court. Advantage is taken of his absence to invade Scotland, and soon the patriotic party there is driven to extremity. The Warden is invited to return, lands at Montrose, retakes Perth, and fights the battle of Black Irnside. Presently the only stronghold in that part of Scotland remaining in English hands is the fortalice of Lochleven.]

Bot in Lochleẅyn thair lay a cumpané,

[1] island.
[2] lay armed.
Apon that inch[1] in a small hous thai dycht[2];

[3] strong.
Castell was nayn, bot wallyt with water wicht[3].

[4] assembled.
Besyd Carraill thai semblyt[4] Wallace beforn;

His purpos was for till assay Kyngorn.

[5] named.
A knycht hecht[5] Gray than captane in it was;

[6] manner.
Be schort aẅys[6] purpos he tuk to pas.

[7] Rather.
Erar[7] he wald bid chalans off his king

Than with Wallace to rakyn for sic a thing.

That hous thai tuk, and litill tary maid.

Vpon the morn, with-outyn mar abaid,

Atour the mur, quhar thai a tryst had set,

Ner Scotlandis Well thair lugyng tuk but let.

Eftir souper Wallace bad thaim ga rest :

"My-selff will walk, me-think it may be best."

[8] without repining.
As he commaundyt, but gruching[8] thai haiff don.

[9] armed.
In-to thar slep Wallace him graithit[9] son,

Past to Lochleẅyn as it was ner mydnycht,

Auchtene with him, at he hed warnyt rycht.

[10] examine.
Thir men wend weill he come to wesy[10] it.

"Falows," he said, "I do yow weill to wyt;

Considyr weill this place, and wndirstand

[11] hurt.
That it may do full gret scaith[11] to Scotland.

Out off the south and power cum thaim till,
Thai may tak in, and kep it at thair awn will.
Apon yon inche rycht mony men may be,
And syn wsche out, thair tym quhen at thai se.
To bid lang her we may nocht wpon chans,
Yon folk has fud, trast weill, at sufficians.
Wattir fra thaim forsuth can nocht be set ;
Sum wthyr wyill ws worthis[1] for to get.   [1] behoves.
Yhe sall remayn her at this port all still,
And I my-selff the boit sall bryng yow till."
Thair-with in haist his weid off castis he :
" Apon yon sid na wachman can I se ;"
Held on his sark, and tuk his suerd so gud
Band on his nek, and syn lap in the flud,
And our he swam, for lattyng[2] fand he nocht.   [2] hindrance.
The boit he tuk and till hys men it brocht,
Arayit him weill, and wald no langar bid,
Bot passyt in, rowit to the tothir sid.
The inch thai tuk with suerdis drawyn in hand,
And sparyt nayn that thai befor thaim fand ;
Strak duris wp, stekyt men quhar thai lay ;
Apon the Sothroun thus sadly semblyt thai.
Thretty thai slew that was in that samyn place ;
To mak defens the Inglismen had no space.
Thar women fyve Wallace send off that sted ;
Woman nor barne he gart neuir put to dede.
The gud thai tuk, as it had beyn thair awyn.
Than Wallace said, " Falowis, I mak yow knawin,
The purẅyance that is with-in this wanys[3]   [3] habitation.
We will nocht tyne[4]. Ger sembyll all at anys,   [4] lose.
Gar warn Ramsay and our gud men ilkane[5] ;   [5] each one.

I will remayn quhill this warnstor[1] be gane :"
Send furth a man, thair horsis put to kep[2],
Drew wp the boit, syne beddys tuk to sleip.

Wallace power, quhilk Scotland Well ner lay,
Befor the son thai myssyt him away.

3 lament.

Sum menyng[3] maid, and merẅeillyt off that cace.
Ramsay bad, 'Ces, and murn nocht for Wallace.
It is for gud at he is fra us went ;

4 verity.

It sall ye se, trast weill, in ẅerrament[4].

5 pledge.

My hed to wed[5], Lochleẅyn he past to se :
Bot that is thar, no Inglisman knaw we
In all this land, betwix thir watters left.
Tithandis off hym ye sall se son hereft.'

As thai about was talkand on this wys
A message com and chargyt thaim to rys.
"My lord," he said, "to dyner has yow cald
In-till Lochleẅyn, quhilk is a ryoll hald.
Ye sall fair weyll, tharfor put off all sorow."

Description of Wallace.

[Wallace surprises Dumbarton and Rosneath, and Douglas
rises in the south and takes Sanquhar. Dundee is the last
strength remaining in English hands in Scotland, and to it the
Warden lays siege. News at this point is carried to King
Edward, then in France. He hastens home and prepares to
invade Scotland with a hundred thousand men. At the same
time the French send a herald to ask if Wallace wishes succour.
With him the herald brings a French description of the hero.]

The wyt off Frans thocht Wallace to commend;
In-to Scotland, with this harrold thai send
Part off his deid, and als the discriptioune
Off him tane thar be men off discretioun,
Clerkis, knychtis, and harroldys, that him saw;
Bot I hereoff can nocht rehers thaim aw.
Wallace statur, off gretnes, and off hycht,
Was jugyt thus, be discretioun off rycht,
That saw him bath dissembill and in weid[1];
Nyne quartaris large he was in lenth indeid;
Thryd part lenth in schuldrys braid was he,
Rycht sembly, strang, and lusty for to se;
Hys lymmys gret, with stalwart pais and sound,
Hys browys hard, his armes gret and round;
His handis maid rycht lik till a pawmer[2],
Off manlik mak, with naless gret and cler;
Proportionyt lang and fayr was his wesage;
Rycht sad off spech, and abill in curage;
Braid breyst and heych[3], with sturdy crag[4] and gret;
His lyppys round, his noys was squar and tret[5];
Bowand[6] bron haryt, on browis and breis[7] lycht,
Cler aspre[8] eyn, lik dyamondis brycht.
Wndyr the chyn, on the left syd, was seyn,
Be hurt, a wain; his colour was sangweyn.
Woundis he had in mony diuers place,
Bot fair and weill kepyt was his face.
Off ryches he kepyt no propyr thing;
Gaiff as he wan, lik Alexander the king.
In tym off pes mek as a maid was he;
Quhar wer approchyt the rycht Ector was he.
To Scottis men a gret credens he gaiff;

[1] unclad and in armour.

[2] palm-leaf.

[3] high.
[4] neck.
[5] long and well proportioned.
[6] Wavy.
[7] eyebrows.
[8] sharp.

Bot knawin enemys thai couth him nocht disayff.
Thir properteys was knawin in-to Frans,
Off him to be in gud remembrans.
Maistir Jhon Blayr that patron couth rasaiff,

1 wrote. In Wallace buk brewyt¹ it with the layff.

Wallace's Meeting with Bruce.

[Wallace defeats the English advance guard of ten thousand
under Woodstock on Sheriffmuir, but, on the eve of encountering
Edward himself, Comyn, brother of the Countess of March, sows
dissension between the Warden and the Stewart. Stewart claims
by virtue of his office to lead the vanguard; Wallace refuses, and
withdraws from action. In consequence, in the great battle of
Falkirk, Stewart is defeated and slain, chiefly by the valour of
Bruce, who fights on the English side. In defending the Scottish
retreat Wallace is wounded by Bruce, and Sir John the Graham
is killed.]

Quhen Wallace saw this knycht to dede was wrocht

2 mastered. The pytuous payn so sor thyrllyt² his thocht

3 nature. All out off kynd³ it alteryt his curage;

4 mad. Hys wyt in wer was than bot a wod⁴ rage.

Hys hors him bur in feild quhar-so him lyst;
For off him-selff as than litill he wyst.
Lik a wyld best that war fra reson rent,
As wytlace wy in-to the ost he went,

5 driving. Dingand⁵ on hard; quhat Sotheroun he rycht hyt,

Straucht apon hors agayn mycht neuir syt.

6 many. In-to that rage full feill⁶ folk he dang doun;

7 was cleared a great space. All hym about was reddyt a gret rowm⁷.

[With difficulty the Scottish troops pass Carron Water, the
tide being in; and Wallace's own horse, having been wounded
falls dead on gaining the further bank.]

To the Torwod he bad the ost suld ryd.
Kerlé and he past wpon Caroun syd,
Behaldand our¹ wpon the south party.　　　　　　¹ over.
Bruce formast com and can² on Wallace cry,　　　² begin.
"Quhat art thow thar?" 'A man,' Wallace can say.
The Bruce ansuerd, "That has thow preẅyt to-day.
Abyd," he said, "thow nedis nocht now to fle."
Wallace ansuerd; 'I eschew nocht for the.
Bot that power has thi awn ner fordon;
Amendis off this, will God, we sall haiff son.'
"Langage off the," the Bruce said, "I desyr."
'Say furth,' quoth he; 'thow may for litill hyr³.　　³ cost (?)
Ryd fra that ost, and gar thaim bid with Beik.
I wald fayn her quhat thow likis to speik.'
The ost baid styll, the Bruce passyt thaim fra;
He tuk wyth him bot a Scot that hecht Ra.
Quhen that the Bruce out off thair heryng wer
He turned in, and this question can spcr:
"Quhy wyrkis thow thus, and mycht in gud pess be?"
Than Wallace said, 'Bot in defawt off the.
Throuch thi falsheid thin awn wyt has myskend⁴.　⁴ mistaken.
I cleym no rycht, bot wald this land defend
At thow wndoys throu thi fals crucll dcid.
Thow hast tynt twa had beyn worth fer mair meid,
On this ilk day, with a gud king to found⁵,　　　⁵ to go.
Na⁶ fyve mylyon off fynest gold so round　　　　⁶ Than.
That euir was wrocht in werk or ymage brycht.
I trow in warld was nocht a bettir knycht
Than was the gud Graym off trewth and hardement.'
Teris tharwith fra Wallace eyn doun went.

[After further bitterly reproaching Bruce for fighting against his own kingdom Wallace retires to his men.]

¹ separated.

Thus thai depertyt¹. The Bruce past his way,
Till Lithqwo raid, quhar that king Eduuard lay,
The feild had left, and lugyt a south the toun,
To souper set. As Bruce at the palyoun
So entryt in, and saw wacand his seit,
No wattir he tuk, bot maid him to the meit.
Fastand he was, and had beyn in gret dreid;
Bludyt was all his wapynnys and his weid.
Sotheroun lordys scornyt him in termys rud,
And said, " Behald, yon Scot ettis his awn blud."
The king thocht ill thai maid sic derisioun;
He bad haiff watter to Bruce off Huntyntoun.
Thai bad him wesche; he said that wald he nocht:
"This blud is myn, that hurtis most my thocht."

² had remorse for.

Sadly the Bruce than in his mynd remordyt²
Thai wordis suth that Wallace had him recordyt.
Than rewyt he sar, fra resoun had him knawin,
At blud and land suld all lik beyn his awin.
With thaim he was lang or he couth get away;
Bot contrar Scottis he faucht nocht fra that day.

Wallace's Lament for the Graham.

Wallace slepyt bot a schort quhill and raiss.

³ manner.

To rewll the ost on a gud mak³ he gais
Till erll Malcom, Ramsay, and Lundy wicht;
With fyve thousand in a battaill thaim dycht.
Wallace, Lawder, and Crystell off Cetoun,

Fyve thousand led, and Wallace off Ricardtoun,
Full weyll arayit in-till thair armour clen,
Past to the feild quhar that the chas had ben;
Amang the ded men sekand the worthiast,
The corss off Graym, for quham he murned mast.

Quhen thai him fand, and gud Wallace him saw,
He lychtyt doun, and hynt[1] him fra thaim aw   1 took.
In armys vp. Behaldand his paill face,
He kyssyt him, and cryt full oft, "Allace!
My best brothir in warld that euir I had!
My afald[2] freynd quhen I was hardest stad!   2 honest.
My hop, my heill[3], thow was in maist honour!   3 covering, defence.
My faith, my help, my strenthiast in stour[4]!   4 storm.
In the was wyt, fredom, and hardines[5];   5 sense, generosity, and boldness.
In the was treuth, manheid, and nobilnes;
In the was rewll, in the was gouernans;
In the was wertu with-outyn warians;
In the lawté[6], in the was gret largnas[7];   6 loyalty.
In the gentrice[8], in the was stedfastnas.   7 liberality.
    8 gentlehood.
Thow was gret caus off wynnyng off Scotland,
Thocht I began and tuk the wer on hand.
I wow to God that has the warld in wauld[9]   9 under sway.
Thi dede sall be to Sotheroun full der sauld.
Martyr thow art for Scotlandis rycht and me;
I sall the wenge, or ellis tharfor de."

Was na man thar fra wepyng mycht hym rafreyn
For loss off him, quhen thai hard Wallace pleyn.

Thai caryit him with worschip and dolour ;

¹ buried. In the Fawkyrk graithit¹ him in sepultour.

[Presently the Scots fall upon the English quarters in Linlith-
gow, put Edward to utter rout, and drive him from the country.
Wallace then assembles the lords at Perth, resigns the Warden-
ship, and retires to France. He is made lord of Guyenne, which
he wins for the French king. But while the envy of the French
leaders is excited by his prowess, Scotland is again over-run by
her enemies. Wallace is implored to come back. Once more he
returns, once more passes through a series of adventures, and
once more sets Scotland free. Then it is that King Edward,
despairing of force, determines upon craft. Sir John Menteith,
Wallace's "gossip," is bribed with gold and promises, and
undertakes the capture. Wallace has invited Bruce to take the
crown, and has been asked to meet the latter privately on
Glasgow moor. He is lying accordingly with a single com-
panion at Robroyston in that neighbourhood when the house is
surrounded at dead of night by Menteith, and through the
treachery of a servant the hero is taken weaponless in his sleep.
He is carried to London, arraigned at Westminster Hall as a
traitor, and executed with all the barbarity of the time.]